HARA-KIRI

HARA-KIRI

Japanese Ritual Suicide

by Jack Seward

CHARLES E. TUTTLE COMPANY
Rutland, Vermont & Tokyo, Japan

Representatives

For Continental Europe:
BOXERBOOKS, INC., *Zurich*

For British Isles:
PRENTICE-HALL INTERNATIONAL, INC., *London*

For Australasia:
BOOK WISE (AUSTRALIA) PTY. LTD.
104–108 Sussex Street, Sydney 2000

Published by the Charles E. Tuttle Company, Inc.
of Rutland, Vermont & Tokyo, Japan
with editorial offices at
Suido 1-chome, 2–6, Bunkyo-ku, Tokyo, Japan

Copyright in Japan, 1968, by Charles E. Tuttle Co., Inc.

All rights reserved

Library of Congress Catalog Card No. 67-11973

International Standard Book No. 0-8048-0231-9

First printing, 1968

Fifth printing, 1981

0239-000145-4615

PRINTED IN JAPAN

To Mother
"God's Greatest Gift"

TABLE OF CONTENTS

Introduction 9

Chapter I SEPPUKU DEFINED 13
Definition 13 • First Eyewitness Account by a Westerner 14 • Changes in Methods of Execution 20 • Breaches of Tradition 21

Chapter II ORIGIN AND TYPES 23
Beginnings of Sacrifice 23 • Early Documents on Seppuku 25 • Seppuku in the Feudal Penal Code 28 • Why the Abdomen Was Chosen 29 • Kinds of Seppuku 32

Chapter III CUSTOMS AND FORMALITIES 41
Sites Used in the Seppuku Ceremony 41 • The Site Itself 44 • Formalities at the Site 46 • The Kenshi 47 • Ritual Procedures 52 • Kaishaku 61 • Degradation of Seppuku 68

Chapter IV SEPPUKU AND SHINJU 73
Definition of Double Suicide 73 • Comparison of Seppuku and Shinju 75 • Germs of Humanity in Battle Records 78 • Disintegration from Within 80 • Decline of Bushido 84 • The Gempuku Ceremony 87 • Criticism by Commoners 88

Chapter V REVIVAL OF SEPPUKU 91
An Imperfect Renovation 91 • Unification of Objects of Loyalty 93 • Speculation About Bushido 94 • Modern Seppuku 94 • Downfall of Bushido 101

Glossary 105

Bibliography 111

Index 113

INTRODUCTION

THE MAJOR purpose of this book is to clarify the historico-sociological background and significance of a unique Japanese method of self-destruction which, by stages during the feudal ages (1190–1867), became institutionalized under the name of *seppuku* and came to be an integral part of the discipline of the samurai, the warrior class. Although seppuku was a form of suicide, it was often awarded to an offender as a form of honorable but necessary punishment. In time, it came to characterize Bushido, the moral code of the warrior class.

The word seppuku is the *on* or Japanese rendering of the Chinese reading of two characters 切腹 meaning "cutting the stomach"; the same two characters, in reverse order, can also be pronounced hara-kiri, and this latter word is more common in spoken Japanese. It is pertinent to comment that the mispronunciations "harry-carry" or "hari-kari" by some Westerners might not be understood by the Japanese.

As we explore ancient Japanese social life and focus our attention on such literature as the poems of the Manyoshu (A.D. 313–759), a collection of the first Japanese poems written utilizing the phonetic values of the imported Chinese characters, we are surprised to find the Japanese a light-hearted people, given to singing and love-making. Further, in the *Kojiki*, a collection of ancient myths compiled in A.D. 712, death is scorned as filthy and gruesome; the death of the goddess Izanami may be cited as an example. According to ancient Japanese beliefs, death was abhorrent. Even today, this attitude toward death characterizes the religion of Shrine Shinto, which is an institutionalized distillation of the ancient beliefs. Therein, nearness to death imparts an uncleanliness that requires ritual purification. Here is an example of a religion that declines to offer funeral services because the priest would be unclean for three days after approaching a corpse. This is exactly as recounted in the Book of Leviticus in the Old Testament (Lev. 21:1). Even though some Shinto priests may compromise and deign to officiate at funerals, their attitude toward funerals remains negative and they would not perform such duties were it not for the most importunate supplications of favored members of their congregation. Even so, the Chief Priest will never officiate.

With the advent of Buddhism to Japan in A.D. 285, brought by Wani, a celebrated Korean scholar possibly of

Chinese descent, the foundations were laid for a gradual shift from an essentially native Japanese view of life, characterized by love of living and shunning of everything concerned with death, to the fatalistic acceptance of death in Buddhism. The simple primitive animism of Shintoism could not withstand the onslaught of the profound philosophy of Buddhism.

In the *Tale of the Genji*, the first Japanese novel to be written in the *kana* syllabary, by Lady Murasaki about one thousand years ago, pathos is the basic undercurrent permeating the entire work. The Japanese nobles depicted in this non-fictional account are not at all like those described in the Manyoshu poems, who leaned toward happy love affairs and gay songs.

Historically, however, the foregoing transition from optimism to fatalism did not engender a general devitalization or effemination of those warriors who fought valiantly in the clash of the Genji-Heike (usually abbreviated as Gem-Pei) from 1180 to 1185. On the contrary, the Buddhist philosophy taught that the mutation of things and the transitory nature of this world call for an attitude of resignation. Such resignation created a death-defying and dauntless attitude on the battlefield.

The Shintoistic beliefs made man positive and aggressive while the life-minimizing, negative views of Buddhism contributed toward making him desperately fearless and bold. Thus these two spiritual elements blended curiously to contribute toward the formation of a moral code of the samurai, which later came to be institutionalized as Bushido, the Way of the Warrior.

In the more than eight hundred years from the time of the *Tale of the Genji* until the close of the feudal age in 1867, this unique method of self-destruction grew to occupy the main coign in the disciplinary code of the samurai and to serve as the keynote in magnifying the concept of honor in the Way of the Warrior.

Bushido had become firmly established in Japan as the Way of the Warrior by the beginning of the long and successful reign of the Tokugawa Clan (1603–1867). Within its framework, seppuku was not only meted out as an honorable sentence of death to violators of certain of the Tokugawa laws but also was practiced to demonstrate and emphasize resistance, remonstrance, loyalty, and affirmation of the correctness of one's position.

How did it develop and how was it applied? It is the task of this work to explore this curious social phenomenon, scrutinizing diverse data and sources to the end of rectifying the often superficial and sometimes fallacious interpretations of scholars and laymen alike, especially in the Western world.

I

SEPPUKU DEFINED

Definition

SEPPUKU is the keynote of discipline in the Japanese code of chivalry. To define it precisely, we should first know why there are two widely used words with the same meaning: seppuku and hara-kiri.

In Japanese society today, the accepted rule is to render official terms in the *on* or Japanese way of pronouncing the original Chinese character, and such is the case with seppuku. The same two characters, in reverse order, can also be read hara-kiri in the *kun* or native Japanese style of pronunciation. The word hara-kiri is used only in conversation, and not for official purposes or in formal speech or writing.

Hara-kiri is mentioned in numerous books written by Westerners. *The Encyclopedia Britannica, Nelson's Ency-*

clopedia, and *Webster's New International Dictionary* carry the word. For example, the last gives:

> **hara-kiri** (ha'ra-kē'rē) *n.* (Jap., stomach cutting). Suicide by the nobles and samurai in case of disgrace, real or fancied, and commanded by the government to certain disgraced officials; disembowelment; —more elegantly called *seppuku*. Written also, but incorrectly, hara-kari.

Many Westerners know this much about the word, but their knowledge about the full and deeper significance of the practice itself is limited. To provide a practical initial introduction, it is pertinent to refer to an account of seppuku written by an Englishman, Lord Redesdale (the former A. B. Mitford), who was Secretary to the British Consulate in Japan in 1868, the first year of the modern era in Japan.

First Eyewitness Account by a Westerner

Through the last years of the Tokugawa Era and into the initial years of that of Meiji, there was much internal strife in Japan between the supporters of the Emperor and the adherents of the Shogun (the *de facto* administrator of the country), especially over the burning question of foreign inroads. During this period of confusion, several incidents hostile to Westerners occurred.

In February of 1868, a number of Japanese soldiers from Bizen fired on the foreign settlement in Kobe, which was then called Hiogo. The responsible Bizen samurai was ordered to commit seppuku. Lord Redesdale was one of the witnesses to the ceremony, and recorded it in his book, *Tales of Old Japan*. An excerpt runs as follows:

> As a corollary to the above elaborate statement of the ceremonies proper to be observed at the *hara-kiri*, I may here describe an instance of such an execution which I was sent officially to witness. The condemned man was Taki-Zenzaburô, an officer of the Prince of Bizen, who gave the order to fire upon the foreign settlement at Hiogo in the month of February, 1868—an attack to which I have alluded in the preamble to the story of the Eta Maiden and the Hatamoto. Up to this time, no foreigner had witnessed such an execution, which was rather looked upon as traveller's fable.
>
> The ceremony, which was ordered by the Mikado himself, took place at 10:30 at night in the temple of the Seifukuji, the headquarters of the Satsuma troops at Hiogo. A witness went from each of the foreign legations. We were seven foreigners in all.
>
> We were conducted to the temple by officers of the Princes of Satsuma and Choshiu. Although the ceremony was to be conducted in the most private manner, the casual remarks which were overheard in the streets, and a crowd lining the principal entrance to the temple, showed that it was a matter of no little interest to the public. The courtyard of the temple presented a most picturesque sight; it was crowded with soldiers standing around in knots round large fires, which threw a dim flickering light over the heavy caves and quaint gable-ends of the sacred buildings. We were shown into an inner room, where we were to wait until the preparation for the ceremony was completed: in the room next to us were the high Japanese officers. After a long interval, which seemed doubly long from the silence which prevailed, Ito-Shunske, the provisional Governor of Hiogo, came and took down our names, and informed us

that seven *kenshi*, sheriffs or witnesses, would attend on the part of the Japanese. [Kenshi means inspector of the corpse.] He and another officer represented the Mikado; two captains of Satsuma's infantry, and two of Choshiu's, with a representative of the Prince of Bizen, the clan of the condemned man, completed the number, which was probably arranged in order to tally with that of the foreigners. Ito-Shunske further inquired whether we wished to put any questions to the prisoner. We replied in the negative.

A further delay ensued, after which we were invited to follow the Japanese witnesses into the *hondo* or main hall of the temple, where the ceremony was to be performed. It was an imposing scene. A large hall with a high roof supported by dark pillars of wood. From the ceiling hung a profusion of those huge gilt lamps and ornaments peculiar to Buddhist temples. In front of the high altar, where the floor, covered with beautiful white mats, is raised some three or four inches above the ground, was laid a rug of scarlet felt. Tall candles placed at regular intervals gave out a dim mysterious light, just sufficient to let all the proceedings be seen. The seven Japanese took their places on the left of the raised floor, the seven foreigners on the right. No other person was present.

After an interval of a few minutes of anxious suspense, Taki-Zenzaburô, a stalwart man, thirty-two years of age, with a noble air, walked into the hall attired in his dress of ceremony, with the peculiar hempen-cloth wings which are worn on great occasions. He was accompanied by a *kaishaku* and three officers, who wore the *jimbaori* or war surcoat with gold-tissue facings. The word *kaishaku*, it should be observed, is the word to which our word *executioner* is no equivalent term. The office is that of a gentleman; in many cases it is performed by a kinsman or friend of the condemned, and the relation between them is rather that of principal and second than that of victim and executioner.

In this instance the *kaishaku* was a pupil of Taki-Zenzaburô, and was selected by the friends of the latter from among their own number for his skill in swordsmanship.

With the *kaishaku* on his left hand, Taki-Zenzaburô advanced slowly towards the Japanese witnesses, and the two bowed before them, then drawing near to the foreigners they saluted us in the same way, perhaps even with more deference; in each case the salutation was ceremoniously returned. Slowly, and with great dignity, the condemned man mounted on to the raised floor, prostrated himself before the high altar twice, and seated himself on the left carpet with his back to the high altar, the *kaishaku* crouching on his left hand side. One of the three attendant officers then came forward, bearing a stand of the kind used in temples for offerings, on which, wrapped in paper, lay the *wakizashi*, the short sword or dirk of the Japanese, nine inches and a half in length, with a point and an edge as sharp as a razor's. This he handed, prostrating himself, to the condemned man, who received it reverently, raising it to his head with both hands, and placed it in front of himself.

After another profound obeisance, Taki-Zenzaburô, in a voice which betrayed just so much emotion as might be expected from a man who is making a painful confession, but with no sign of either in his face or manner, spoke as follows:—

"I, and I alone, unwarrantedly gave the order to fire on the foreigners at Kôbé, and again as they tried to escape. For this crime I disembowel myself, and I beg you who are present to do me the honour of witnessing the act."

Bowing once more, the speaker allowed his upper garments to slip down to his girdle, and remained naked to the waist. Carefully, according to custom, he tucked his sleeves under his knees to prevent himself from falling backward; for a noble Japanese gentleman should die falling forwards. Deliberately, with a steady hand, he took the dirk that lay before him; he looked at it wistfully, almost affectionately; for a moment he seemed to collect his thoughts for a last time, and then stabbing himself deeply below the waist on the left hand side, he drew the dirk slowly across to the right side, and, turning it in the wound, gave a slight cut upwards. Through this sickeningly painful operation he never moved a muscle of his face. When he drew out the dirk, he leaned forward and stretched out his neck; an expression of pain for the first time crossed his face, but he uttered no sound. At that moment, the *kaishaku*, who, still crouching at his side, had been keenly watching his every movement, sprang to his feet, poised his sword for a second in the air; there was a flash, a heavy, ugly thud, a crashing fall; with one blow the head had been severed from the body.

A dead silence followed, broken only by the hideous noise of the blood throbbing out of the inert heap before us, which but a moment before had been a brave and chivalrous man. It was horrible.

The *kaishaku* made a low bow, wiped his sword with a piece of paper which he had ready for the purpose, and retired from the raised floor; and the stained dirk was solemnly borne away, a bloody proof of execution.

The two representatives of the Mikado then left their places, and, crossing over to where the foreign witnesses sat, called on us to witness that the sentence of death upon Taki-Zenzaburô had been faithfully carried out. The ceremony being at an end, we then left the temple.

The ceremony, to which the place and the hour gave an additional solemnity, was characterized throughout by that extreme dignity and punctiliousness which are the distinctive marks of the proceedings of Japanese gentlemen of rank; and it is important to note this fact, because it carries with it the conviction that the dead man was indeed the officer who had committed the crime, and no substitute. While profoundly impressed by the terrible scene, it was impossible at the same time not to be filled with admiration of the firm and manly bearing of the sufferer, and of the nerve with which the *kaishaku* performed his last duty to his master. Nothing could more strongly show the force of education. The Samurai, or gentleman of the military class, from his earliest years learns to look upon the *hara-kiri* as a ceremony in which some day he may be called upon to play a part as principal or second. In old fashioned families, which hold to the tradition of ancient chivalry, the child is instructed in the rite and familiarized with the idea as an honorable expiation of crime or blotting out of disgrace. If the hour comes, he is prepared for it, and gravely faced an ordeal which early training has robbed of half its horrors. In what other country in the world does a man learn that the last tribute of affection which he may have to play to his best friend may be to act as his executioner?

The foregoing account is a typical example of seppuku in its most honorable form, imposed as a sentence of death. Inasmuch as a criminal is actually executed, it is, significantly, a form of the death penalty. The criminal, however, is permitted to take the initiative and to strike the first blow toward his own death. As such, seppuku is also a form of self-punishment and expiation and was granted only to those who, though violators of certain codes or regulations, were nonetheless worthy of the respect of those determining the penalty. On occasions, the condemned man was regarded with warm sympathy and his regrettable but necessary passing was honored by a solemn ceremony such as the one witnessed by Lord Redesdale.

The events in the foregoing narrative by Lord Redesdale

occurred, as noted, in 1868, when feudalism was beginning to give way to the modern era. Yet, for the most part, the feudal system was still intact and at its most highly developed stage. Accordingly, the seppuku seen by Lord Redesdale was perhaps the penultimate point of the formalized ceremony itself. Although practiced at the beginning of the Tokugawa Era 268 years before the Meiji Restoration in 1868, seppuku was not nearly as stereotyped and rigidly ceremonialized then as in the case witnessed by Lord Redesdale.

Changes in Methods of Execution

In ancient Japan, we do not find any evidence of decapitation as a method of execution. One piece of indirect evidence is that the sword of this period was straight and designed for piercing, not for cutting. It was during the Gem-Pei strife that the slightly curved sword with a cutting edge was first used in battle on a large scale. Even as late as the beginning of the period of Gem-Pei fighting, there is the example of Minamoto-no-Tametomo who, defeated in battle and desperate, plunged his short sword into his stomach and then, still alive, withdrew the blade and stabbed himself again, this time cutting into his spinal column. Had the custom of *kaishaku* (assisting at seppuku) been developed then, he would not have had to make the second and fatal cut himself. With the Gem-Pei Period, more efficient methods of execution and self-destruction began to develop in Japan. Prior to that, strangulation and burning were probably the common modes of execution and of suicide.

Breaches of Tradition

The samurai was devoted to the code of chivalry and lived for the cause of honor, according to his own lights. To have his own name—his escutcheon—besmirched was the supreme stultification to the warrior. As he tried to live with honor, so his superiors tried to accord him an honorable method of death when his crime, though proscribed, was not a dishonorable one. There were, however, exceptional cases where contemptuous and insulting methods of execution, though generally condemned, were applied to samurai.

There was the time when Tokugawa Ieyasu, the founder of the Tokugawa Regime, captured an enemy general and, instead of permitting him to commit seppuku, ordered him decapitated. Historians record this unusual breach of tradition as a stain on the reputation of this great administrator.

Toyotomi Hideyoshi, the general who preceded Tokugawa Ieyasu as the *de facto* ruler of Japan, also committed a similar breach when he ordered Ishikawa Goemon, an infamous bandit and the son of a samurai, boiled to death in oil. In this instance, however, the punishment was meted out to Ishikawa as a bandit and his near-samurai status availed him naught.

Too, during the early Tokugawa Era, Catholics were

often crucified, regardless of whether they were samurai or commoners. This persecution can be attributed more to fear of rumored Spanish political and military inroads than to dislike of this alien religion.

In spite of the rare exceptions, however, cruel and unusual methods of execution were seldom meted out to samurai.

II

ORIGIN & TYPES

Beginnings of Sacrifice

THE ORIGIN of immolation is hidden in a nebulous prehistoric time when primitive men believed that a form of human life extended beyond the grave. In their belief, the spirit of the deceased was very desirous of gathering the beloved ones left behind unto himself. Hence, the spirit was often exceedingly feared by ancient Japanese. The ancients, therefore, put huge stones on the burial spot so that the spirit would not come out to haunt the living in a dream or in the shape of a ghost. The custom of immolation originated at such a stage in civilization. Beloved wives, concubines, servants, and even horses were buried with the deceased, so that he might keep on "living" peacefully and comfortably in the nether world, which was called in Shintoism, *yomi*.

The custom of immolation was later transformed into a type of self-immolation called *hito-bashira*, which means a "human pillar." When a bridge was washed away in a flood, when a new bridge was found most difficult to build, or when a large structure such as a castle was feared for its weak foundation, the ancient people speculated that it was due to the displeasure of deities of the water or earth. In that event, a human sacrifice or a "human pillar" was sometimes made. Later it became an established custom. Just whom to choose and by what method formed the basis of many tragic stories.

More than 30 years ago breaks were discovered in the inner wall of the Imperial Palace, the former Tokugawa Edo Castle, near where a tower is located. A thorough excavation was made in connection with the repairs and workmen found ten human skulls and accompanying bones.

There is an old legend in Japan about a certain village chief whose name was Iwafuji. The villagers had to select a man to become a "human pillar" in building a bridge which was washed away frequently and which caused the village much distress. Iwafuji hit upon a capital idea. It was this: the first man who happened, the next morning, to pass the spot where the bridge stood in ruin would be offered as a sacrifice to the deity of the river. The village elders agreed. As Iwafuji was very excited with his own idea, he came out early the next morning to see who would be the victim. The village elders came soon thereafter and contended unanimously in loud voices, "Ye, Iwafuji, shalt offer thyself, because ye hast come the first." And so it was.

Early Documents on Seppuku

In the sixth year of Meiwa (1769), a short composition concerning seppuku was indited by Taira Teijo, who also called himself Ise Anzai. According to him, there is no record of seppuku in Japan's oldest chronicles, the *Kojiki* and *Nihon Shoki*. In these chronicles and in other histories immediately following them there are, however, frequent references to suicides, which were usually accomplished by self-strangulation or burning one's self to death by setting fire to one's house.

In the *Hogen Monogatari* (*Tales of the Hogen Civil War* in 1156), there is recorded an account of Minamoto-no-Tametomo who, at the age of 28, disemboweled himself after furious fighting on behalf of a lost cause, leaning against a pillar in his house. Since death was slow in coming, he hastened its advent, before the enemy could catch and abuse him, by cutting into the nerve centers of the spinal column. This is probably the *first* example of seppuku found in Japanese chronicles.

Whereas the *Hogen Monogatari* was written between 1185 and 1190, when seppuku was already known among many samurai, some scholars say that there might be an anachronism in this narrative. However, considering that there was an interval of more than twenty years between the occurrence and the writing, it is not difficult to imagine that such a valiant warrior as Tametomo might have desired to show his valor by utilizing seppuku and that it was practiced with increasing frequency over the following twenty years. His ignorance of the easier method to finish seppuku by cutting the carotid artery, as was learned later, rather than the excruciating cutting into the spinal nerve center, may well serve to indicate that his act of seppuku, if not the very first, was at least one of the first such cases, since it was carried out in such a primitive fashion.

Another example in the *Tales of the Hogen Civil War* is the narrative about Naiki-no-Heita who committed seppuku in the following manner: When Minamoto-no-Tameyoshi was killed in the Hogen fighting, Otowaka, his child of thirteen, and three other children were beheaded the following day. The youngest of these children was called Tenno, and was seven years of age. Right after the decapitation of this child, his guard, Naiki-no-Heita, clasped the child's headless body to him in a fit of passionate grief and committed seppuku, saying how painful it would be to live on—remembering his young master's fate—and that he had better die to follow his master.

In a painting of a scene from the Go-Sannen-Gassen (Three-Year War, 1086–89), there is an incident of seppuku depicted. Yamano Shotaro, in his book on the subject of suicide, comments that it is possible that the artist included the seppuku scene in view of the established custom in his own time rather than in the time of the War. The conclusion of the Go-Sannen-Gassen was 67 years prior to the Hogen Civil War. Therefore, the picture's scene would be considerably older than Tametomo's seppuku.

Ten years after Tametomo's suicide, Minamoto-no-Yorimasa, wounded and defeated in battle, entered Byodoin Temple (in Uji, south of Kyoto) to execute the same deed. Sitting on his fan and leaving a poem of farewell, he pressed the point of a long sword to his abdomen, and, leaning forward, forced the blade into his body. This method of seppuku became the acceptable style soon thereafter.

During the so-called Yoshino Era, furious battles were often fought between the cliques of the two reigning Emperors. This era lasted from 1336 to 1392. When the Hojo military regime (which succeeded the Genji) was overthrown by an army sent by Emperor Godaigo, it seemed that peace had come to the Kyoto Regime, centered, as it was, around the Emperor. But, with the rebellion of Ashikaga Takauji, the Emperor had to flee to Yoshino, south of Kyoto, where he established a government that administered the neighboring areas and vowed eventually to extend its sway over the entire country. On the other hand, Ashikaga enthroned a new Emperor, chosen from among the kinsmen of the Imperial Family. Thus two Emperors reigned simultaneously. The regime in Kyoto was called the Hoku-cho, or North Court, and the one in Yoshino was called the Nan-cho, or South Court.

In a 40-scroll chronicle called *Taiheiki*, stirring stories are recounted about samurai who ended their lives bravely by seppuku during numerous encounters between the adherents of the two courts:

Toki-no-Juro. Cutting his abdomen, he turned toward the north* and then succumbed.

---

*It is the Buddhist custom to place a corpse with its head to the north. This ceremonial custom derives from the belief that Buddha entered Nirvana facing the west with his head to the north and his right arm underneath his head.

Murakami Yoshiteru. Realizing that his master, Prince Morinaga, must either escape from their desperate last stand or commit suicide, Murakami determined to sacrifice himself for his master. He climbed to the top of a tower of the citadel and shouted down to their foes below, "Behold, I am Prince Morinaga. Watch with your eyes what I do!"

Removing his outer garment, he made a deep straight cut across his abdomen from left to right. Then, pulling out a handful of his intestines, he flung them against the wooden side of the tower and putting his short knife point-first into his mouth, fell forward on his face.

Kusunoki Masashige. When Kusunoki, a devoted adherent to the cause of Emperor Godaigo, lost a battle against the overwhelming forces of the Ashikaga at Minatogawa (Kobe) in 1336, he and his brother, Masasue, committed mutual suicide by piercing each other with their long swords.

Kusunoki Masatsura. When Masatsura, son of Kusunoki Masashige, lost the battle at Shijo-Nawate against the powerful army of the Ashikaga and immolated himself for the cause, 32 faithful retainers followed him in seppuku.

Seppuku in the Feudal Penal Code

The death penalty down to the time of the Ashikaga was carried out by two methods, strangulation and decapitation. Late in the Ashikaga Period, seppuku was added to honor the condemned. Other judiciary documents at that time, however, make no discernible mention of seppuku and suggest that the custom as an honorable method of execution was only in the formative stage toward the end of the Ashikaga Period.

With the advent of the Tokugawa Period, the government decided to formalize all phases of the social system and the following five grades of penalties were instituted for the samurai class:

1. *Hissoku*—Contrite Seclusion. This penalty was subdivided into three parts: restraint, circumspect prudence, and humility.
2. *Heimon*—Domiciliary Confinement. This was subdivided into two: 50 days and 100 days.
3. *Chikkyo*—Solitary Confinement. This was subdivided into three: confinement in one room, temporary retirement, and permanent retirement (till death).
4. *Kai-eki*—Attainder. Permanent removal of the name of the offender from the roll of the samurai.
5. *Seppuku*

Why the Abdomen Was Chosen

The word *hara* or abdomen has a common root with the word *hari* which means tension. Ancient Japanese associated tension in the abdomen with the soul. The abdomen is the place where the soul resides; the more vital the action, the greater the tension. At the same time, it is the physical center of the body; hence they were led to look upon the abdomen as the cradle of one's will, thought, generosity, boldness, spirit, anger, enmity, etc.

There are many Japanese idioms that are associated with the word *hara*. For example:

hara ga tatsu, literally, "the stomach stands up," meaning to become angry.

hara o watte hanasu, "to talk over a matter with an open stomach," meaning to have a frank talk.
hara no okii hito, "a person with a big stomach," meaning a generous man.
hara-guroi hito, "a person with a black stomach," meaning a sly man.
kare no hara o yomenai, "I cannot read his stomach," meaning "I do not understand what is in his mind."
hara o kimeru, "to determine one's stomach," meaning to make up one's mind.

The reference to the abdomen in such expressions is not a monopoly of the Japanese. In Greek we have *phren*, primarily "diaphragm," also "seat of passions and affections"; hence, "heart," "mind," "understanding," or "reason."

In French *ventre* (abdomen) is often associated with *coeur* (heart, mind). *Entrailles* means both intestines as well as feelings, tenderness, heart, or pity.

In English, we use idioms like "he has no stomach for the task," "intestinal fortitude," or "the pit of one's stomach," etc.

In Hebrew, the word *rahmim* in the plural means the intestinal part of the body, or womb, and also has the meaning of affection. For example, in Genesis 43, we find, "His [Joseph's] heart yearned toward his brother." In the original Hebrew, this is given as "His bowels grew hot toward his brother."

In still other verses as Proverbs 12: 10, Amos 1: 11, First Kings 3: 26, the same term is used to designate "pity," "grace," or "favor."

Still, it was the Japanese who devised a manner of sui-

ORIGIN & TYPES 31

cide that cuts into the soul or the center of the emotions, and their peculiar cultural philosophy found justification in the act.

Considering the interpretation of the abdomen as the soul-center, it would seem the most proper place of the body for suicidal purposes, expiating the crime as well as purging the shame.

Too, seppuku being a very painful method of suicide, commoners would likely refrain from it and only persons of great determination would undergo the ordeal. Judging from the fact that the Zen sect of Buddhism suddenly emerged to gain the favor of the samurai class from the Kamakura Period on (that is, from the beginning of the feudal age), there is good reason to infer that the act of seppuku was associated with the austerities and self-mortification of Zen.

According to Zen doctrine, Buddha-hood is achieved only after acts of austere self-mortification. It is a state that must be actively pursued and won by the individual. Thus, the ordeal of seppuku would give high merit toward the attainment of Buddha-hood.

Proof that the condemned man could endure severe hardships would further contribute toward alleviating the gravity of his offense in the eyes of the public and of posterity.

Finally, the samurai attached great importance to the manner of dying and to the moment of death. According to their code, the death sentence of simple decapitation brought eternal shame to the memory of the warrior. In seppuku, however, the samurai died of his own accord, at least in the ritual sense, and this was a fitting end to a valiant life.

Kinds of Seppuku

There are several classifications of seppuku, based on the motive for the act, its method of execution, and the degree of severity of the offense. For example, when the act of seppuku was motivated by a sense of loyalty to the daimyo or lord, it was called *chugi-bara*. *Chugi* means loyalty and *bara* is a contraction of hara-kiri (pronunciation of the word *hara* often changes in a compound). *Chugi-bara* included both self-immolation on the death of one's master (*junshi*) and for the purpose of remonstration (*kanshi*).

The custom of self-immolation that became fashionable during the Edo Period makes us aware of the tight, cruel bonds of the feudal system. In the case of Otani Sampei, the sandal carrier, his strong reluctance to die is most touchingly expressed in his farewell verse which said, "I am reluctant to die, indeed I am. This being my lot, I regret that my lord was so gracious to me." Here, the self-immolation was prompted by strong social pressures. There certainly might have been some people who gladly immolated themselves; on the other hand, some might have been compelled to do so by the auto-suggestive vainglory of Bushido; or, as was the case with Otani Sampei, some were no doubt urged on to reluctant deaths by the opinion of society.

In some cases, the lord and his principal retainers may

have encouraged such immolators under the concept that, the more immolators, the greater and stronger the clan. Mass psychology is contagious. Among many retainers the thought prevailed that it was better to die by immolation than of old age and, in so doing, to improve the standing of one's children. All through the eras of Genki, Tensho, and on down to Keicho, this spell-binding practice increased. After the death of a lord, from three or four to as many as twenty vassals often died and this fashion held sway for over 70 years!

Junshi was inspired by the affection and loyalty for their lord in the retainers who protected them and their descendents. This doleful custom had once been abolished in the early stages of Japanese history. When the Empress Hihasu-hime passed away in A.D. 3, Nomi-no-Sukune, the most favored vassal of the court, counseled the Emperor to condemn the traditional custom of self-immolation on the part of the deceased's retainers. The conscientious servant had asked 100 potters from his home province of Izumo to make clay dolls resembling men and horses and offered these to the Emperor. Pleased with Sukune's wisdom, the Emperor issued an Imperial edict prohibiting self-immolation by retainers and ordered that these clay dolls, called *haniwa*, be substituted for the human beings and animals that had been buried with deceased nobles up to that time. In recognition of his suggestion, Sukune was awarded a name of honor, Haji-no-Omi, and the edict put an end to the unpleasant practice for several hundred years.

The custom of immolation, once stopped by Nomi-no-

Sukune, seems to have passed into the nebulous world of legend. But the rise of the samurai class during the furious strife between the Genji and Heike clans again called the ancient, quiescent custom to life in a different form, that is, *self*-immolation. Loyalty was emphasized, but this did not necessarily mean the slavish attachment of a dog. It held out the hope of a full life in the role of a vassal. When one loses his master, it means that he has lost a vital part of his life. This relationship was beautified to the extent that formularized acts of self-immolation came to be accepted. It was held that there is nothing so laudable as for a vassal to die for his benevolent master.

Buddhism also contributed to the advancement of the custom of self-immolation. According to the teachings of Buddhism, the relationship between the parent and the child is "one world," that is, this life; that of a couple is "two worlds," the former life and this life. According to the theory of *karma*, on the other hand, the relationship between the master and his vassal is "three worlds," that is, the former life, this life, and the future life. This fatalistic *karma* philosophy inspired the Japanese warriors to gladly offer their lives at the proper moment for their masters.

During the Muromachi Period (1392–1573), however, we do not see very many examples of self-immolation for one's master. After passing through the dark century called the "Warfare Period," the long-lasting Tokugawa Era was ushered in. It was during this period that we see a grand display of self-immolation and even the strong Edo Government had great difficulty in quenching this fever.

When a period of peace began with the Keicho Era (1596–1615), many of the warriors who fought so valiantly on the battlefield were still alive. Life became rather dull for them; there was something wanting, for there were no means to show loyalty to the lords and to distinguish themselves. This situation brought forth many examples of self-immolation on the occasion of the death of a great lord.

According to the *Kodokan Kijutsu Gi* written by Fujita Toko in the 19th century, cases of self-immolation began increasing in number about the time of the Warfare Period. It was not an unnatural act as long as wars prevailed; however, there are numerous recorded incidents that point out the horrible and unnatural practice that it was during times of peace.

These incidents show how it was the fashion of the day to sacrifice one's self for his lord. This was called by another name, i.e., *oibara*, which means "following or accompanying hara-kiri." Since this custom was highly lauded, vassals were encouraged to sacrifice themselves to pass on fine reputations to their descendants.

Later, however, from the Gem-Pei Period on, self-immolation was most often practiced by the samurai when a warrior's master fell on the battlefield.

Ieyasu, the first Shogun of the Tokugawa Government (1600–1867) came strongly to oppose the custom and voiced his distaste for it in his "Legacy" or posthumous instructions, the 76th article of which read: "Although it is undeniably the ancient custom for a vassal to follow his lord in death, there is not the slightest reason for this practice. Confucius himself ridiculed the making of *yo* [effigies buried with the dead]. These practices are strictly forbidden to secondary as well as to primary retainers. He who disregards this prohibition is the reverse of the faithful servant. His descendants shall be punished by the confiscation of his property as a warning against any who would disobey this law. . . ."

Finally, the *bakufu*, or feudal government, was obliged to issue a harsher edict. It was a futile custom. It would be far better to serve loyally the survivors of the dead lord. It should be an act of disloyalty to waste a precious life in the master's service through such sacrifices. Under this principle the *bakufu* prohibited the custom as of May 23rd, the 3rd year of Kambun (1663). The edict of prohibition, which directed that the family of any violator be punished, ran as follows:

> We have said long before that the act of self-immolation is both evil and futile. However, it has not until now been officially prohibited. We see too many vassals immolate themselves these days. In the event that a lord has a presentiment that a certain vassal is liable to immolate himself, he should admonish him strongly against it during his lifetime. If he fails to do so, it shall be counted as his fault. His heir will not escape appropriate punishment.

It is said that the man who recommended this prohibition was Lord Matsudaira Nobutsuna of Izu.

Even prior to this edict, there were a few daimyo, or lords, who banned this custom in their own fiefs. For example, when Lord Hotta Masamori decided to immolate himself for the third Shogun, he said to his vassals before his death that he himself would follow his Shogun-master in death but that his own vassals were by no means to follow him; that, instead, they should live to serve his sons.

Five years after the ban, on February 19th in the 8th year of Kambun (1668), there occurred a violation. A case of self-immolation took place in the house of Okudaira, the lord of Utsunomiya Castle. The *bakufu* judged that it was the fault of the lord. However, in view of the fact that the house of Okudaira had distinguished itself in the service of the Shogunate and taking into account the great favor shown to this feudatory by the Third Shogun, the penalty was mitigated. Still, this feudatory was degraded and ordered to move to a lesser fief in Yamagata.

Against the family of Sugiura Uemon no Hyoei, a self-immolator, the following adjudication was pronounced: the eldest son (Zen'eimon) and the second son (Yokota Hichijuro) shall commit seppuku; the two daughters' husbands, Okudaira Godayu and Inada Sebei, shall be banished.

Finally, in 1682, in addition to the *bafuku* edict, a prohibitory clause was added to the penal code of the samurai class, putting an end to the custom. Thus the infraction of the clause by General Nogi and his wife on the eve of the funeral of Emperor Meiji in 1912 caused considerable commotion among the Japanese, for they assumed the General to be a model of ancient chivalry and a strict adherent to the samurai code.

Junshi or self-immolation to follow one's master in death thus finally ceased. In place of it, a person who wanted to honor his deceased master decided to renunciate this lower world, and take the tonsure and become a monk to pray throughout his life for the soul of his dead master.

An outstanding example occurred when Minamoto-no-Sanetomo was assassinated beside the gingko tree in the Hachiman Shrine in Kamakura (1219). Then, about one hundred retainers renounced this world and became monks or nuns.

Kanshi, attempts to remonstrate with an erring superior by committing seppuku, were made now and then but not quite as often as *junshi*.

Oda Nobunaga, the famed general, was a wild youth. His closest retainer committed seppuku to caution him and thus occasioned deep self-reflection by Oda.

Sokotsu-shi, or expiatory seppuku, meant "death for imprudence or heedlessness." In the event of a grave mistake, the samurai shouldered his responsibility and committed seppuku in expiation. This kind of seppuku was practiced frequently during the Tokugawa Period when social institutions had become formalized and rather stereotyped. Even unintentional breaches of formalities, therefore, often served as cause for expiatory seppuku.

In the post-feudal era, suicide as a means of taking responsibility did not cease among the Japanese. Such tragedies occurred among the locomotive engineers on the Imperial train of the Emperor Meiji, when minor delays were construed as heedlessness and responsibility was taken by committing suicide.

During World War II, a young naval reserve officer, a graduate of a commercial college, committed seppuku when he could not complete his assigned task within the given period of time. He was greatly honored at his funeral by the Japanese Navy. Such seppuku was deemed expiatory and all trace of shame was removed. No Japanese would laugh at such a deed. Even now, Japanese use the idiom *seppuku-mono*, which means "a situation that calls for seppuku."

Seppuku is also resorted to as a means of displaying dire resentment, hatred, or enmity. This type is called *munen-bara*, or seppuku from mortification. For example, Sen-no-Rikyu, a celebrated teacher of the tea ceremony at the time of Hideyoshi, offended the latter to the extent of being ordered to commit seppuku. Angered at the unjustness of the charge, he cut open his abdomen and drew out part of his intestines, which he placed on a tray. He cut them free of his body and, dying, instructed that they be presented to Hideyoshi. This kind of *seppuku* is also called *funshi*, seppuku caused by indignation.

Although there is no precise word for it in Japanese, a sort of "vicarious seppuku" was practiced during the Sengoku Jidai (The Era of Warfare) with the aim of saving the lives of many by the sacrifice of one life, often that of the most responsible person. For example, when Hideyoshi was warring with Mori Motonari, he decided to try to effect a reconciliation with the latter. At that time, Hideyoshi had under siege one of Mori's castles, which was commanded by Shimizu Muneharu. Hideyoshi offered to spare the rest of the garrison if Lord Mori would have Shimizu commit seppuku, to which Mori agreed.

Connected to this episode is a moving example of *junshi:* On the eve of Shimizu's seppuku, his favorite vassal

Shirai sent a request that Shimizu visit his room. When Shimizu arrived, Shirai apologized for having his master visit his humble quarters and explained that he had wanted to reassure his master that seppuku was not difficult and that he, Shimizu, should not be concerned about what he would have to do on the morrow. So saying, Shirai bared his abdomen to show that he himself had completed the act of seppuku only a moment before Shimizu's arrival. Shimizu gave Shirai his deepest thanks for his loyal devotion and assisted him in *kaishaku*, i.e., he beheaded him with his sword.

III

CUSTOMS & FORMALITIES

Sites Used in the Seppuku Ceremony

IN THE earlier part of the Tokugawa Period, seppuku rites were carried out in temples.

In 1647, a vassal of a certain feudal lord ended a quarrel with a sailor by killing him. The magistrate of Osaka, after investigating the case, ordered that the offender commit seppuku in Osaka's Kanzanji Temple.

Again, in 1644, during the Shoho Era, a samurai was ordered to commit seppuku for the crime of highly immoral behavior. The site used was in the Shimpukuji Temple in Kojimachi, in Edo (Tokyo).

On the 26th of June in the 8th year of Empo (1680), a Buddhist grand mass was being observed for Ietsuna, the late Shogun, at the Zojoji Temple in Edo. At that time, Sir Nagai, the Lord of Shinano, was killed by Sir Naito, the

Lord of Izumi, with whom he was on bad terms. The latter was taken as a prisoner immediately by officials of the Shogunate. Several days later, he committed seppuku at the command of the Shogun in the courtyard of Shinryuji Temple.

In all of the foregoing examples, attention should be directed to the fact that a Shinto Shrine was never used. This derives from the Shinto belief that corpses are anathema to holy precincts and priests, whereas in Buddhism, the whole structure of holy writ is directed toward preparation for death. Hence, the Buddhist temples were ideal sites for the seppuku ceremonies.

When the seppuku rite was carried out in the provinces, away from the Shogun's seat of government in Edo, there was little concern that it in any way might displease the Shogun. However, when it took place in Edo, there was a greater chance of incurring the anger of the Shogun for one or another of the complicated rules of etiquette by which the nobles lived.

Under the Tokugawa Shogunate, there were about 60 feudal lords, great and small, throughout the country. These lords were not permitted to live permanently in their own fiefs but had to maintain mansions and spend much of their time in Edo. They could not stay in their own fiefs longer than one year at a time and, even then, they had to leave their wives and children in Edo during their absence from the capital. This strategy on the part of the Shogun had certain controlling effects: Each lord could not stay in his own fief long enough to adequately prepare for and foment rebellion; his family were hostages in the Shogun's capital; and the great expenses of going to and from the capital in the highly elaborate processions of the day and of maintaining separate residences at home and in style- and class-conscious Edo often left the lords without excess funds with which to rally their men and stir up émeutes.

This being the situation, each lord and his family had to spend much of his time in residence in Edo, under the ever vigilant eyes of the Shogun and his constabulary, and they had to pay every possible attention to not offending the Shogun.

For example, Lord Inoue once commanded that one of his vassals, Ishikawa Katsuzaemon, commit seppuku at the Lord's mansion in Kanda-bashi, which was located just a relatively short distance from the castle of the Shogun. When the news of this seppuku reached the ears of the Shogun, it displeased him very much, because he did not feel that the sentence was justified. He therefore ordered Lord Inoue to move his residence farther from his own castle, under the pretext that seppuku without Shogunal sanction, committed so close to the castle, was a sign of disrespect.

Thereafter, those lords with residences near the castle saw to it that all cases of seppuku for which they were responsible took place in villas outside the capital or in homes in the distant suburbs.

When an offense calling for the sentence of seppuku took place while a lord was traveling with his retinue, it was deemed proper to borrow a nearby Buddhist temple for the ceremony.

The Site Itself

Toward the latter half of the Tokugawa Era, the seppuku ceremony usually came to be performed in the evening. The ceremony took place usually in the mansion or garden of the feudal lord where the condemned was being kept under surveillance. The decision as to whether the ceremony was to be conducted indoors or in the yard was based primarily on the social standing of the offender.

For offenders of comparatively high rank, the size of the place of disembowelment was 36 square *shaku*, the *shaku* of those days being about 14 inches. There were entrances on both the north and the south. The north gate was called the *shugyo-mon* (ascetic gate) and the south gate, the *nehan-mon* (Nirvana gate). Two white-edged *tatami* (reed mats) were arranged to form the figure "T."

A white *futon* (cushion) about four feet square was placed on the *tatami*. At the four corners, poles were erected and surrounding curtains were hung from these. Right in front of the two *tatami* was a gate approximately 9 feet high and 7 feet wide. It looked like the entrance gate leading into the premises of a temple; in this case, however, it was a green bamboo frame covered with white cloth. From the framework were hung white curtains. Four white streamers called *mujoki* (banners of heartlessness) were flown from the tops of the four corner poles. These banners were to be carried with the corpse to the tomb after the ceremony.

At dusk, two lamps, one on each side of the *tatami*, were

lit. These lamps were placed on calyxes supported by long bamboo poles and covered with white cloth. The person to commit seppuku, entering through the "ascetic gate," sat on the prepared cushion, facing north. At the same time he passed through the entrance, his *kaishaku* (assistant) came in through the opposite south gate and sat on the *tatami* prepared for him beside the victim.

If it was not the yard, a seldom-used room was usually selected as the site for the ceremony. Selection of the living room or another room in frequent use as the site signified more respect for the person to commit seppuku.

For all that, it was a common and understandable desire to wish to avoid unnecessary mess from the blood and some were of the opinion that a new, simple structure should be built for each case of seppuku and destroyed later. In some fiefs, rooms for the special and sole use of the seppuku ceremony were constructed. Remains of the latter can be seen today in the famous castle of Himeji.

Thus, on one hand, there was the human feeling of abhorrence of blood and, on the other, the theoretical notion that seppuku exemplified the flower of Bushido or chivalry and should thus be revered. There was a case in point of the Forty-Seven Loyal Retainers, the famous samurai who avenged their lord's death and who were all ordered to commit seppuku by the Tokugawa Shogun. It was arranged that 17 of these would perform the ceremony within the inner premises of the mansion of Lord Hosokawa Tsunayoshi. His vassals were concerned about the possible defilement of the premises and they were arranging for a purification ritual to be performed by a *shugenja* (an ascetic hermit of the mountains) from the Shinzoin. When he heard of this, Lord Tsunayoshi ordered that his vassals desist. It was his opinion that these 17 samurai had been granted an honorable way of death and that their crime, if crime it was, came from their observing such precepts of Buddhism as "Honor thy Master." Therefore, he felt that the seppuku of the 17 samurai on his premises would serve more to propitiate the Buddhist tutelary deities rather than to offend them, and that there was no need for purification rites.

Formalities at the Site

After the beginning of the 19th century, the dimensions of the seppuku site were fixed at 18 square *shaku* in all cases. The person to commit seppuku sat facing the *kenshi* (inspector). The first duty of the *kenshi* was to assure himself that all preparations were in order. After this, he so informed the custodian, called the *rusui-yaku*, who, in turn forwarded this information to the caretaker (*azukari-nin*). It was the office of the custodian to guide the condemned from the room of his confinement to the site of the ceremony. The *kenshi's* next function was to pronounce the sentence. He began with the following announcement:

"I hereby pronounce the supreme command of the Shogunate."

Thereafter, he would read the sentence:

"Considering the charge that ——— [name of the condemned] did ——— [the offense for which he is to be punished], the subject is herewith commanded to commit seppuku."

Thereupon, the person ordered to commit seppuku bowed and uttered briefly but respectfully a few words of gratitude for having been given this honor. Then the seppuku rite itself began, performed as was recorded by Lord Redesdale.

When seppuku was performed in a room, five folds of white cotton cloth were piled upon the two *tatami* which were indispensable for the occasion. In the event that the entire room was covered with the matting, its surface was shielded by a scarlet felt covering to prevent blood from staining the *tatami*.

Other preparations included obtaining a coffin, a box for the decapitated head, and a wooden bucket. These were concealed behind a plain white *byobu* or standing screen.

When the seppuku rite was performed in the garden of a mansion or in the open, thick straw mats were used to cover the immediate surrounding area. Lacking these, sand was spread over the site.

The Kenshi

The *kenshi* or inspector is the highest functionary officiating at the ceremony of seppuku. When a samurai under the surveillance of a lord by order of the *bakufu* (Shogunate government) was adjudicated guilty and told to commit seppuku, a notice is sent from the *rochu* (feudal cabinet) to the caretaker, containing the information that on a certain day and at a certain time a *kenshi* will be sent. This notice is sent at night.* On receiving this unofficial notice, the custodian, that is, the formal representative of the caretaker, has to return a letter of acceptance.

The *kenshi*, who is under direct command of the Shogun, is accompanied by an associate *kenshi*. The *kenshi* for such occasions is chosen from among lords who belong to the Shogun's direct feudatory.

To the senior *kenshi* is attached one *ometsuke* (a supreme judge), while to the associate *kenshi* is attached one *metsuke*, next to the former judge in rank. In addition, two lower-ranking *metsuke* and four to six constables will follow the *kenshi* group. When the *kenshi* are taken from the lower grades of samurai, judges and constables of appropriate rank are appointed. Needless to say, the *kenshi* must be received as supreme envoys, that is, as direct messengers from the Shogunate.

Prior to the visit of the ranking messenger, an officer who could be described as an "auxiliary *kenshi*" shall visit the mansion for surveillance or preliminary inspection. His duty is to note the general condition of the place for the contemplated ceremony, prepare a chart of the mansion, list the names of those who will participate in the ceremony, etc.

It is up to the caretaker to take advantage of this op-

---

*The reason why this portentous notice was forwarded at night is that it was believed that such news of doom should not defile the morning (or auspicious) hours of the day.

portunity to consult the inspector whether the *kaishaku* (the second or assistant) should be selected from among his own men. In the event that the inspector supplies the assistant, he will be chosen from among his attendants, probably from among the lower *metsuke*. However, if the latter have not had an audience with the ranking Shogun, the assistant will be chosen from among the *doshin* or constables.

If the assistant is to be chosen from among the men of the household to which the condemned has been given in custody, then it is due process for the inspector to interview that person, paying proper attention to his character and especially to his qualifications in the art of swordsmanship.

When all preparations are in order, the supreme envoy will make his appearance. This officer is presented only to the seppuku performer, and not officially to the caretaker. Therefore, it was the custom to forward an unofficial notice of arrival to the caretaker, requesting him not to come out of his manor to greet the inspector. Only when such notice was not sent was it considered proper to appear for greetings.

Upon arrival of the inspector, a receptionist shall step out of the vestibule, while the daimyo together with his *karo* or principal retainers await in deep obeisance within. The receptionist will reverently receive, at the entrance, the inspector's long sword* on a piece of purple crepe, and then follow him while another receptionist ushers him into a parlor. Other followers are led to a waiting hall.

---

*It was customary for samurai to carry two swords, one long and one short.

The inspector's group will never be provided with any food or drink until the ceremony has been completed.

When the death sentence is to be pronounced, both the senior and associate inspector as well as their followers will prepare themselves by putting on the two swords officially required.

Simultaneously with the arrival of the advance notice of the inspector's coming, the condemned is informed of the same. Thereupon, the condemned begins his preparations, with the aid of the household, by dressing his hair and bathing.

A kimono bearing his family crest and a ceremonial surcoat called a *kamishimo* are brought to him on a tray when he has finished bathing. After dressing, he is led off by a chief samurai who wears only a *wakizashi* or short sword. (Precautions are taken so that the condemned man cannot snatch away the long sword of his guide.) On both sides as well as in back of the condemned will walk six guards. At the threshold of the room, the man to die leaves his guide and guards to turn toward the inspector. Then, the supreme command of doom is pronounced. As soon as this duty is accomplished, it is often the case that the senior inspector leaves the mansion. In this event, the associate *kenshi* will remain to watch the actual act of seppuku.

Prior to bidding farewell to this world, the condemned man will change his garb for the third and last time to a snow-white outfit symbolizing purity and the decision to end his life.

The participants in the seppuku rite are one or two *karo* or principal retainers, two or three samurai, one caretaker-official, six guards, one *kaishaku* and his two assistants, one incense-bearer who need not be a samurai, and a Buddhist priest if the rite takes place in a temple. For the task of burial as well as cleaning up the polluted ground or room, four men are selected from among the *ashigaru*, the lowest grade of samurai, whose functions were menial. These served on this occasion without their swords.

During the performance of the ceremony, the inspector may either lay his long sword at his side or wear it, whichever he likes. After he has inspected the decapitated corpse for his subsequent attestation, he is supposed to leave the site. Only when he is a person of high rank may he carry the long sword in his left hand; if not, he must bear it in his right. Such were the minutiae of manners. When the sword (in sheath) is held in the left hand, it is easier to draw, while difficult when held in the other. Such reasoning often decided feudal manners.

When seppuku is to be committed in a courtyard, the inspector will be dressed in an outfit called the *kataginu* which is comprised of the *kamishimo* and the loose trousers called the *hakama*. Wearing two swords, he is seated on a stool, signifying his post as the supreme commander for the day.

When the duties of the inspector are completed, both the senior and his associate, if they are together, shall visit, on their return route, the mansion of a *rochu* (feudal cabinet member) assigned to such duty to report that the inspectors have completed without incident the supervising of the final disposal of the condemned. Since this *rochu* will be expecting their visit, candles will be burning in the parlor where he will utter the stereotyped response, "It was an unavoidable act."

As can be seen, the customs and formalities surrounding the ceremony were extremely complicated. One major reason for this was that ranks and grades, as well as corresponding manners and formalities, were excessively emphasized for the purpose of keeping peace and order among the tough and warlike samurai.

Ritual Procedures

When a high-ranking samurai was placed under the custody of a certain noble, it usually, although not always, meant that he would be commanded to perform seppuku. The retainers of the custodian noble had, therefore, to be most attentive and cautious so as to prevent untoward occurrences and, at the same time, not give the doomed man the certain foreknowledge of his pending sentence.

Often this custodial period lasted several days or longer. In the case, however, of Lord Asano Takumi-no-Kami, it was about four o'clock in the afternoon that he was placed in the custody of Lord Tamura and he was sentenced to death that same evening. This was a rare case and one of the most dramatic incidents during the Tokugawa reign. It took place when His Imperial Majesty's messenger was visiting the Tokugawa castle, where a great fete was to be held. Lord Asano was appointed by the Shogun to officiate at the grand reception. On the other hand, the expert director of manners and ceremonies was

Kira Kozuke-no-Suke who, probably because Lord Asano did not give him "tea money" or a bribe *sub rosa*, failed not only to instruct the latter adequately but even taught him to wear a certain costume on the wrong occasion: where long dragging trousers were to be worn, Lord Asano was told to wear *hakama* or short trousers. When he emerged thus clad in the grand corridor, he was shamed to find all the other lords wearing long trousers. When he next met Kira within the palace, the quick-tempered young Lord Asano tried to kill him but, being prevented by guards, achieved only a slight cut on Kira's forehead. Then he shouted, "Kira, wait!" and threw his short sword at Kira, hoping thus to inflict more serious injury. Unfortunately, this short sword pierced the gorgeously decorated golden sliding door at the end of the *Matsu-no-Roka* (Pine Corridor), and this incident was the cause behind the Shogun's command that Lord Asano commit seppuku. This story has since been made into a kabuki play, *Chushingura*, or the "Treasury of Loyal Retainers."

When a samurai was put under the surveillance of the lord he served or into the custody of his kinsmen, the responsible party had to prepare attendants both to take care of him as well as to watch over him. These watchmen had to pay keen attention not to offend the confined man nor to excite him. If he should ask if he would be commanded to commit seppuku, they were to answer simply that they knew nothing about it.

As the day for the seppuku ceremony approached, the condemned man's family, friends, vassals, and messengers from his master were permitted to visit him.

Three days prior to the date set for seppuku, close friends were invited to a farewell banquet. The custodian of the condemned had to arrange the affair so that the doomed man would cause no disturbance or trouble. All through the banquet there was no mention made of regret or sorrow, resigned resolution being taken for granted. At this farewell party, all guests were requested to sit to the left of the condemned man, to give him this last honor. The Japanese believe that the right side is the position of honor.

Japanese in those days ate at individual tables or on small raised trays called *o-zen*. The *o-zen* placed before the man to commit seppuku was distinctly different from the others. It was called *tachi-oshiki* and was a thin wooden plate with four long legs. As a rule, all the dishes were vegetarian. However, if the departing man was a lord or a person of high rank, he was allowed to break the vegetarian rules and his dishes were served on an ordinary black-lacquered *o-zen* covered with clean, white paper. Three slices of spicy pickled vegetables were indispensable; "three slices" in Japanese is rendered *mikire* which could also mean "to cut flesh." Here is a portentous play on words.

Sake (rice wine) was served to the left, or contrary to the normal order. The small cup, called a *choku*, should be filled to the brim in two pourings, so as to avoid the meaning of repetition implied by the number three. Symbolism permeated the banquet from beginning to end. Similar topics of conversation were not to be brought up twice. The chopsticks used at this dinner were made of anise wood or bamboo, the former being used exclusively for funeral dinners. Thus, the doomed person was made to feel that he was already, in a sense, being mourned.

When the banquet was over, the caretaker came in and announced, "The date for your seppuku has been set on the ———; as to the *kaishaku-nin* [the assistant at seppuku], ——— has been appointed, so please take note," etc. Without losing any time, the assistant came in and said, "I am the man appointed as the *kaishaku-nin;* if you have any wishes, please let me know." The assistant *kaishaku-nin*, also made his obeisance and said, "I am the assistant *kaishaku-nin;* please do not hesitate to ask for anything you desire." Next, it was time for the seppuku performer to say what he wanted done. If there was nothing, he would say so. If he wanted to arrange the precise moment of decapitation, he would say that he would make a signal, such as raising his right hand.

It was sometimes the case that in the actual ceremony, the *kaishaku-nin* himself became so excited that he gave the *coup de grâce* before the seppuku performer gave any signal. Both the performer and the assistant should be of one mind to accomplish a clean, final cut at the right instant.

If the condemned man could leave everything up to the assistant, who should be a reliable swordsman, it was much easier for both. When the famous 47 *ronin* committed seppuku, it was the concern of the authorities not to let them suffer any pain. Thus, no sooner had the seppuku performer stretched out his hand to take the knife than the highly qualified *kaishaku-nin* decapitated him with one clean cut. In such cases, it was not construed as a mere execution because the condemned man took the initiative in reaching for the seppuku knife.

The technique of *kaishaku* was precise and delicate. Therefore, the discussion after the banquet between the seppuku performer and the *kaishaku-nin* was of major importance in achieving a laudable ceremony that would be recounted by following generations.

The farewell greetings were all so ceremonialized and stereotyped that they served as some relief at such a doleful time. In reply to the command to commit seppuku, the condemned man would answer, "My crime should have deserved a more severe punishment, whereas I have been allowed to commit seppuku, for which my gratitude is boundless," etc. The caretaker and other intimate persons would also give their last greetings. The exact phrases would differ with the individual as well as with the circumstances. However, the content would generally be like this: "This is the day for you to commit seppuku. The weather is fine and the day is auspicious. I hope you will be able to accomplish seppuku without any difficulty." After hearing these messages, the seppuku performer would reply, first to the caretaker for his kindnesses, "I heartily thank you for your troubles during these days and for your cordial treatment." To the inspector and other officials, the doomed man would say, "I appreciate your good offices; I am ready to commit seppuku in a few moments."

He would then proceed to the place of the ceremony. There, he would again solemnly bow to the assistant, uttering a few words of appreciation; the same would be accorded to the other guards.

When all had been said, the seppuku performer would receive a cup of plain water, which was called *matsugo-no-mizu* or "water for the last moment." The vessel was either a regular tea cup or a small dish of unglazed pottery, which was brought in on a white offering tray (*sambo*) by, if available, the chief priest of the temple of which the condemned man was a member. At that moment, the priest would deliver a short sermon after which the condemned man drank the water. The last cup of water also served to calm the nerves of the man facing death.

After the priest had carried the cup back to his seat, one of the officials would produce the knife on the *sambo*.

On some occasions, sake was served. While the seppuku performer was seated at his place ready for the act of seppuku, servants would bring in small two-layer dishes of unglazed pottery containing three slices of spiced pickled vegetables and *kombu* (kelp or seaweed). The chopsticks were placed contrary to the usual direction and the sake bottle was held in the left hand and poured to the left. The ceramic dish for sake was filled in two pourings, and was drunk in two swallows and then two more; that is, in four swallows altogether. The Japanese words for "four" and "death" are pronounced the same, *shi*.

The seppuku knife was not long. In the first place, a long knife would be dangerous. It might happen that the condemned man would suddenly change his mind and decide not to die. Were he an excellent swordsman, he might use a long knife or sword to effect his escape. It once happened that the condemned man snatched up the sword of the *kaishaku-nin*, whom he killed with one blow, and fled.

The standard length of the knife for seppuku was 0.95 *shaku*, or about eleven and a half inches. It was wrapped in two folds of a Japanese tissue paper called *sugihara* paper, leaving the point exposed slightly over half an inch. When the crime was particularly reprehensible, twice that length was bared. It was wrapped in an inverted direction and tied at three points. The cutting edge was laid facing the seppuku performer with the point to his left.

If the seppuku performer asked to use his own knife, it was the principle not to comply with this request. The *kaishaku-nin* would make excuses, such as the desired knife was not at hand, or it would take time to obtain the approval of the *bakufu* government to use it. In the event there were delays, it would not give the samurai a good reputation after death, which most samurai were concerned about. If the seppuku performer was a man of high rank or if he were dying for a popular cause, his wish was granted, but the blade of the knife was deliberately dulled.

The *sambo* or white wooden tray on which the knife was carried was placed backwards before the condemned. Two corners of the rim of the tray were cut to make a depression to hold the knife and prevent it from slipping off the tray. According to the earlier custom, the seppuku performer bared himself entirely from the waist up. Later, however, the kimono was only partly opened at the front without being completely lowered.

The preparation of the white standing screen as well as

cleaning up after the ceremony was the office of the *ashigaru* samurai.

As soon as the seppuku performer opened his kimono, he stretched out his right hand to seize the knife. Without allowing a moment's delay, he cut into his abdomen from left to right. It was counted more courageous to make a slight cut upwards at the end, which was called the *jumonji* or crosswise cut. The exact moment of decapitation was arranged beforehand and the assistant had to know whether or not the condemned would make a crosswise or straight cut. He might either raise his hand or say in a low voice, "*Kaishaku!*"

The *kaishaku-nin* sat about four feet to the left and in back of the seppuku performer, holding himself ready, resting on his knees and toes. The inspector would then say, "*Kaishaku-nin*, maintain your silence," and he would bow reverently.

While handing the knife to the seppuku performer, the *kaishaku-nin* would pick up the sword with his left hand and would place it flat on the *tatami* with the haft to the right. Then, when he had unsheathed the blade, he would lift his right knee, keeping his left foot in place. He poised the sword in air, adding his left hand to the haft and measuring a straight line between the big toe of his right foot and the earlobe of the seppuku performer. Then he made the downward slash toward the lower margin of the hair on the back of the victim's neck.

It was considered expert not to cut the head completely off in one stroke, but to leave a portion of uncut skin at the throat, so that the head would not roll away but would hang down, concealing the face. This technique was called *daki-kubi* or "retaining the head," and was taken as proof of excellent swordsmanship. The *kaishaku-nin* would later make the last separation at leisure, either with the same long sword or with his short knife.

When decapitation was completed, the *kaishaku-nin* took some white tissue paper from his kimono—ten to twenty sheets folded in triangular form. Holding them in his right hand, he placed the head on them, holding the head by the hair and showing it to the *kenshi* for his inspection. The point of the triangular white paper was toward the inspector. If the head was bald, a small blade called a *kozuka* was used to hold the head in position by driving it into the left eye. The head was then placed as close to the neck as possible and the paper used to wipe the sword clean was placed beside the corpse. Sheathing his sword, the *kaishaku-nin* devoutly bowed to the deceased and retired. Then the assistants drew the curtains.

It sometimes happened that the *kaishaku-nin* lost his composure or nerve and was unable to fulfill his role. In such a case, his assistant immediately took his place.

If the seppuku performer was a man of high rank, the head might be sent to relatives. Then the hair was well combed, scented, and the head wiped clean of blood. If the eyes were open, they were closed. If the eyes would not stay closed, they were sewn shut with hair from a horse's tail. These attentions were called *kubi-shozoku* or "head-dressing." The dressed head was wrapped in a square of white cloth and placed in the conventional cylinder-shaped box. In case white cloth was not available, the white kimono of the deceased might be cut up and used as a substitute.

If the head was not to be sent somewhere, it was attached to the body with a ladle-handle containing two holes. The corpse was placed in the coffin on the cushions used by the deceased and sent to the temple where he was registered. The final procedures differed according to local customs.

Kaishaku

The word *kaishaku* means "to attend," "to look after," or "to serve." In the course of time, this term came to be used solely to refer to the act of helping a samurai in committing seppuku and lessening his long drawn-out agony. During the Warfare Period, there were many cases of *kaishaku* to help shorten the period of agony after disembowelment. It was, however, from the time of the fourth Shogun, Tokugawa Ietsuna, during the Empo Era (1673–81) that *kaishaku* was officially established as a part of the seppuku ceremony. In the course of time, even the assistant himself came to be designated by the same word.

The basic motive of *kaishaku* was one of mercy, at least from the viewpoint of the feudal code of the samurai. Though seppuku was considered the flower of Bushido or chivalry, it was believed needless and even cruel, except on the actual battlefield, to let the disemboweler suffer lengthy agony. Thus, *kaishaku* was officially approved and introduced into the seppuku ceremony.

Whatever the standing or rank of the *kaishaku-nin*, the seppuku performer had to follow his orders, although there were customs and standards varying with the rank and offense of the condemned.

The *kaishaku-nin* was expected not to excuse himself from performing this duty. Errors, clumsiness in swordsmanship, or lack of dignity, while not absolutely disgraceful, could detract from his reputation. Young samurai were most likely to make slips. If a senior samurai recommended in his stead a younger samurai solely to escape this onerous duty, it was considered to be an act of cowardice.

Earlier it was pointed out that the finest technique in *kaishaku* was to leave an uncut portion of skin at the throat to "retain the head." Herein lies the philosophy that distinguishes seppuku from mere decapitation. To be decapitated without the seppuku ceremony was a great dishonor to a samurai, because it was the punishment usually meted out to commoners.

The sentence of decapitation was given to such criminals as arsonists, bandits, murderers (for an ignoble cause), and persons guilty of crimes against the state. It was to make a clear distinction from these crimes that the rite of seppuku was initiated. Hence, it was important to employ a swordsman of the highest order so that the head would not be cut off completely at the first blow. For all that, it was nevertheless difficult to always "retain the head." In an attempt to succeed at this difficult task, persons appointed as *kaishaku* prepared for it with two exercises: lopping off the lower halves of leaves on low tree branches, and knocking off a head-like object placed on top of a sand bag.

The costume of the *kaishaku-nin* varied. If the seppuku performer was of high rank, the *kaishaku-nin* wore a new *kamishimo* which was the most formal attire. This applied to his subordinates as well. If the seppuku performer was of medium rank, the *kaishaku-nin*, together with his subordinates, wore only *hakama*. For a lower-ranking man who held neither remarkable status nor office, the aforementioned formalities were not observed by the *kaishaku-nin* or his subordinates. However, when an inspector was sent, all the officers had to be dressed in *kamishimo*, irrespective of the status or crime of the condemned.

Some authorities on seppuku customs said that if the rank of a seppuku performer was high, the *kaishaku-nin* should be dressed all in white and the haft of his sword should be covered with white cloth. In pursuance of this old advice, it became customary for the sheath and haft of the *kaishaku-nin*'s sword to be white in color.

If seppuku was performed within a house or building, the *kaishaku-nin* tied up both legs of his *hakama*. If the rite was to be in a courtyard, the *hakama* was tied up as high as the knees.

As has been noted, the correct timing in the performance of *kaishaku* depended greatly on the swordsmanship of the appointed person.

It was the logical order for the *kaishaku-nin* to use his sword at the proper moment just after disembowelment was completed. However, it was also often the case that decapitation was performed at the moment when the condemned man merely picked up the dirk from the *sambo* tray.

The *kaishaku-nin* had to understand the mentality of the seppuku performer. If he looked like a weak-willed person, the assistant should behead him before he thrust the dirk into his abdomen. However, if a previous agreement was made for decapitation to be done at the very instant when the dirk has been drawn to the right side of the abdomen, then the *kaishaku-nin* should respect that last desire. Still, if the seppuku performer looked as if he were in agony although the cut was incomplete, the *kaishaku-nin* should act immediately. Intent scrutiny was required of him.

To allay possible criticism later, it was recommended as a good precaution for the assistant to have a word beforehand with the inspector and tell him that he might hasten or delay *kaishaku* according to the courage, reputation, etc., of the seppuku performer.

When a young boy was commanded to commit seppuku, it was considered merciful and proper for the *kaishaku-nin* to help him at the earliest moment, i.e., when he picked up the dirk from the *sambo* tray.

In regard to the timing of the death blow, there were three systems of classification. The first system gives three moments when *kaishaku* should be performed:

1. The moment when the seppuku performer stretches out his hand to pick up the dirk from the *sambo* tray.
2. The moment just before the seppuku performer thrusts the dirk into his abdomen.
3. The moment when the seppuku performer stabs the dirk into the left side of his abdomen.

The second system gave four proper moments:

1. The moment when the subordinate who delivered the dirk on the tray was withdrawing.
2. The moment when the seppuku performer began to draw the tray toward him.
3. The moment when the seppuku performer picks up the dirk.
4. The moment when the seppuku performer was about to stab himself.

The third system gave nine permissible moments:

1. The moment when the seppuku performer draws the *sambo* toward him.
2. The moment when the seppuku performer bows after picking up the dirk.
3. The moment just after he stabs himself.
4. The moment when the seppuku performer has drawn the dirk to his navel.
5. The moment when the seppuku performer has drawn the dirk to the right side of his abdomen.
6. The moment when the seppuku performer is about to make the crosswise cut.
7. The moment when the seppuku performer is halfway through the crosscut.
8. The moment when the seppuku performer completed the crosscut.
9. The moment when the seppuku performer withdraws the dirk from his abdomen and places it on his right knee.

The last example was followed in the case described when Lord Redesdale was one of the witnesses at the event.

The *kaishaku-nin* should be an alert watchman. Close

attention to his task was a prime requirement. He had to watch constantly the eyes and feet of the seppuku performer. He could not afford to feel sympathy for the condemned—doing so would be contrary to the spirit of Bushido.

If the condemned man secretly planned to escape, he might involuntarily reveal his intent with his glances or by frequent shifting of his feet. Therefore, even though the seppuku performer might be a close friend of the *kaishaku-nin*, a careful scrutiny of the movements of his eyes and feet was not to be neglected.

Regardless of the relationship of the *kaishaku-nin* to the condemned, he was expected to look upon the seppuku performer as an enemy. If the condemned planned to escape, he might snatch up the sword of the *kaishaku-nin*. To prevent this, the *kaishaku-nin* had to watch constantly his longer sword (*tachi*) as well as his shorter one (*wakizashi*). He was advised not to carry his swords in his hands but to attach them to his belt in the manner called *otoshizashi*.

The cord on the sword-sheath was not to be wrapped around the haft, because it sometimes became coiled around the blade. It was to be tied to the rear.

The *kaishaku-nin* had to be sitting down when the *kenshi* appeared, so he had to take care not to let his limbs become numb, especially on cold days. Even though a man of high rank might be present, he was not to forget to exercise his limbs. Such a precautionary measure was not counted as disrespect.

In addition, regardless of the temperature, the palms

of the hand were liable to become sweaty, and the *kaishaku-nin* was expected to keep them dry.

The *kaishaku-nin* also had to make precise measurements beforehand, so that his sword would not touch the ceiling or the walls when executing his downward stroke.

To eliminate further hindrance to his movements, the *kaishaku-nin* would loosen his *kataginu* or wing-pointed formal surcoat, dropping it off his shoulders.

It was common knowledge among swordsmen that the human neck is about four *sun* long, or a little over four inches, both in the front and rear portions. However, as it varied somewhat with the individual, the *kaishaku-nin* considered it part of his duties to study the length of the neck of the condemned.

There were three positions for holding the sword: high, middle, and low. If the seppuku performer were a person of high rank, it was deemed proper to use the high position. If he were of equal rank with the *kaishaku-nin*, the middle position was recommended.

If the seppuku ceremony were to be held in a courtyard covered with white sand, the *kaishaku-nin* was requested to wear *zori* or straw sandals. However, it was not good form to wear them up to the actual spot for seppuku. Even this etiquette surrounding the *zori* was taken as a delicate indication of the culture and character of the *kaishaku-nin*, and, therefore, could form the basis for criticism.

If the seppuku performer indicated hesitance to carry on with the ceremony, he was sometimes given a *suzuri* or Japanese ink-pot (for use with a writing brush) and told that he might leave a written message. Understandably, he might wish to postpone death, even for a moment. While concentrating on what to write, he would become somewhat calmer. Then, when the victim's neck was in the right position, the *kaishaku-nin* would do his duty. In utilizing this device, however, prior consultation with the *kenshi* was thought to be advisable.

Whenever any conversation was directed at the *kaishaku-nin* by the seppuku performer, "Put your mind at rest" was the stereotyped response usually given. Indulgence in conversation might only serve to further disquiet the mind of the condemned.

According to one school, it was taboo for the seppuku performer to face either east or north for the reasons that the east is the direction of birth and facing the north would show disrespect to the Emperor.

In individual feudal fiefs, the condemned was prohibited from facing the castle, and, within the castle, from facing the main building. Whereas the directions which the condemned could face were west and south, it sometimes happened that the castle or main building was located in one of those directions. In such cases only, the east and north became permissible.

Degradation of Seppuku

In the course of time, the rite of seppuku took on many forms. The wooden sword and the white fan came into use. Of course, these methods were used in the case of crimes which could not be punished in the more honorable way as well as in the case of the lower grades of samurai. However, Yamaoka Shummei, deploring the abuse of the true spirit of genuine seppuku, wrote in his *Seppuku Jisatsu Kojitsu no Koto* (Old Facts about Seppuku and Suicide):

> We have these days an established manner of seppuku using the *kaishaku-nin* in a way which renders use of the dirk unnecessary. A fan is placed on the *sambo* tray; when it is picked up, the seppuku performer is instantly decapitated. It doesn't matter whether he knows how to disembowel himself or not. Such cannot be called seppuku, but only decapitation.

The forms of these quasi-seppuku are as follows:

Sensu-bara or "Fan Hara-kiri." Instead of the seppuku dirk, a fan is placed on the *sambo* tray. The condemned might have been decapitated for his crime but, being mitigated one degree, he was permitted this "imitation seppuku." It might be more proper to classify this as ranking between seppuku and decapitation.

The fan to be used was prepared in this manner: its rivet was removed and the two major stays broken; the entire fan was held together by only a paper string. The traditional Japanese idea is that the fan symbolizes a blessing and happiness because of its ever widening shape. This shape cannot be held without the rivet and the two retaining stays. Hence, for the purpose of seppuku, this symbol of blessing was distorted.

Mizu-bara or "Water Hara-kiri." Originally two small, unglazed dishes were colored gold, silver, vermilion, and green, and were brought to the condemned. When he had poured the water from the upper dish into the one underneath while holding them high in a prayerful posture, his head was cut off.

Later, exactly when is uncertain, this rite also was abbreviated, so that just one unglazed earthenware dish was set forth, without any water. In this case also, the symbolism was marred by chipping the rim of the dish. Even this simple, chipped dish, substituted for the seppuku dirk, saved the face of a samurai.

This "water hara-kiri" was inferior in grade to "fan hara-kiri," and, therefore, was closer to decapitation. The reason for chipping the rim of the earthenware dish was simply to show that a new one, i.e., a sign of benediction, was not used. While the condemned held this dish on his right knee, his head was cut off.

At this level of punishment, however, either *kamishimo* (including surcoat and *hakama*, loose trousers) or just the *hakama* were allowed, depending on the rank of the condemned. It was like standard seppuku, however, in that the same *tatami* were used and the *kaishaku-nin* was dressed the same.

Te-bara or "Hand Hara-kiri." *Te-bara* was alternatively called *yubi-bara* or "finger hara-kiri," *toshu*, or *soe-bara*. This penalty was just under *mizu-bara*, and only slightly higher than mere beheading. Whereas the condemned should have been decapitated, his punishment was mitigated for some consideration by one degree. In this case, he was not allowed to sit on regular *tatami*, but on a thin matting called *usuberi*, a kind of rush mat, while he wore only a plain white kimono. The man who performed the function of *kaishaku* was not called by that name, but rather *tachi-tori* or sword-taker, and this was not considered to be a job for a regular samurai. The *tachi-tori* was chosen from among the *ashigaru* class; he wore a plain, white kimono, the skirt of which was tucked up behind. His striking posture was also less formal; he waited at the right side of the condemned to take advantage of a favorable moment to strike.

Uchi-kubi or "Beheading." *Uchi-kubi* was also called

morokubi, meaning the whole head. Among the three forms of beheading, this penalty ranked the highest in treatment received. The seriousness of the crime was indicated by the choice of place of execution: the premises of the house where confined, at a temple, or in an open field. The criminal was not bound. If his relatives requested the corpse, it would be handed over to them.

Kiri-ume or "Cut Off and Bury." This punishment was limited in its place of execution to a forlorn field. If bound, the criminal was released at the time of execution. A pit was dug, and, as soon as he was beheaded, the body was kicked into it for burial.

Kiri-sute or "Cut Off and Throw Away." The criminal was executed on an out-of-the-way plot of wasteland and his body left exposed on the ground. This punishment was sometimes called *uchi-sute*, also meaning "cut off and throw away."

Shibari-kubi or "Beheading While Bound." This was actually the same as *kiri-ume* except that the criminal was bound at the moment of beheading. Moreover, he was buried still bound.

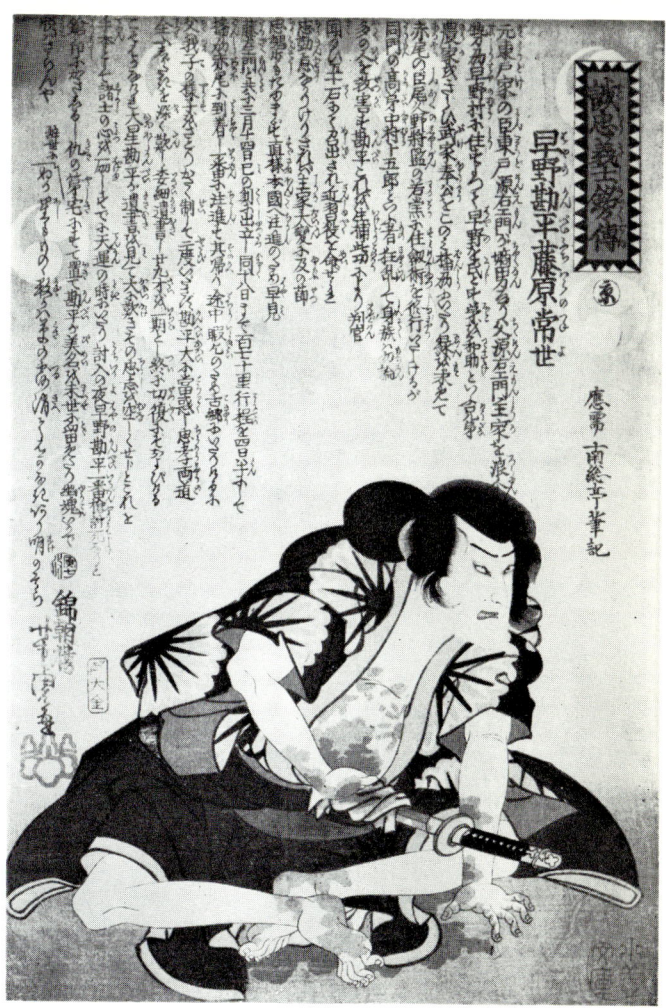

The story of the 47 *ronin*, who are buried in Tokyo, is the source of many theater dramatizations, notably on the kabuki stage. On these pages are woodblock prints of famous kabuki actors in seppuku scenes: above, the dramatized seppuku of one of the *ronin*.

Above: A highly dramatic scene from a play about a famous Tokugawa magistrate in which he has offered to commit suicide. While the *kaishaku-nin* (right) stands ready to draw his sword, a messenger (left) bursts into the room and stops the seppuku. These being mere dramatizations, the seppuku rites are not as described in the text.

Previous Page: "Chushingura" (Treasury of Loyal Retainers) is the most famous kabuki play based on the story of the 47 *ronin*. The print shows the scene where Lord Asano attacks his tormentor (upper half) which led to Asano's sentence of seppuku (lower half). *Kabuki prints courtesy of Waseda University Tsubouchi Memorial Theater Museum.*

IV

SEPPUKU & SHINJU

Definition of Double Suicide

SHINJU in Japanese literally means "inside the heart." More fully, it implies that if the heart were cut open, there would be found only devotion to one's lover; thus, "revealing-the-heart death."

To understand this particular method of self-destruction, it must first be noted that it was an age when contact between men and women was almost completely banned, except in the case of married couples. This was an unwritten law, and both samurai and commoners were under irresistible social pressure to obey it. The function of the woman was not to make love or have romance, but to give birth to heirs of the family. Hence, the vulgar saying: "The womb of a woman is a borrowable vessel." It is curious that such a vulgarity originated under these conditions of stern separation of male from female. Confucianism was responsible for bringing forth such a social ethic. Confucianism teaches, "The male and female shalt not sit together even at the seventh year." The whole relation between men and women was colored with this concept. Under the iron rule of feudalism, it was unalterable. Romance or elopement could mean death by fire or crucifixion. Such a social system sooner or later had to produce violent reactions.

In *Tale of the Genji* written by Lady Murasaki a thousand years ago, there were numerous stories of romance enjoyed by the Japanese of those days before the influence of Confucianism began to be felt. But, in the Edo Period, the only place where one could have free contact with women were the officially licensed gay quarters called *yukaku*, wherein the women were owned by the establishment or "house" and could be visited after payment of a fee. Even in such quarters, only sex—not love—was allowed. However, it sometimes did happen that men and women fell in love, even in houses of ill-fame. When such girls fell in love, they secretly sent letters protesting their devotions to their sweethearts or tried to demonstrate their feelings by avoiding carnal intercourse with other guests or even sometimes cutting off their little fingers and sending them as tokens of their love.

Sometimes, when their love was thwarted at every turn, the lovers resorted to suicide to "reveal the heart." Properly, the word was *shinju-shi*, but *shi*, meaning "death," came to be omitted. This manner of suicide spread among the townspeople very quickly, and the latter part of the

Edo Period came to be characterized by this phenomenon. Many stories of *shinju* remain to this day in the form of novels, dramas, and songs.

Comparison of Seppuku and Shinju

It would be a misinterpretation to think that *shinju* was the *chonin's* imitation of the samurai's seppuku. There is considerable antithesis therein.

The age was outgrowing seppuku and much that it stood for. Feudalism remained as a meaningless formalism that was suffocatingly inhuman. Voices of opposition from the common people began to make themselves heard. They were under the subjugation of the sword but they were learning that no power on earth has any control over death. The common people found a certain elevation of apperception was required to commit *shinju* and a new truth was discovered in so doing. The *chonin* were finding in *shinju* what the samurai had found in committing seppuku: the sense of joyful fulfillment in sacrificing one's life for an ideal, however mistaken or foolish that ideal might be. They were finding in *shinju* a worthwhile death.

Shinju came to be praised and exalted in the literature of the day. In a sense, *shinju* served to expose the shallowness and excessive formality of seppuku and hastened its end.

The adherents of seppuku brought forth the following arguments to show the superiority of seppuku over *shinju:*

1. Seppuku required an admirable mental attitude of

composure, while the approach to *shinju* was characterized by faltering and hesitation.

2. The seppuku knife was the sacred emblem of the samurai spirit, while the "weapon" used to bring about *shinju* was often only the red cord women used to tie around their waists. (This was used to tie the two lovers together when they threw themselves into rivers, waterfalls, or the sea.)

3. *Shinju* was often prompted by the exposure of the ignoble crime of adultery.

4. *Shinju* was often an escape, a fleeing from the pain of living without one's lover. Seppuku, however, was done in fulfillment of one's duty to one's code and class*.

Whereas seppuku could be described as the crowning culmination of Bushido and perhaps of the feudal society from which it grew, *shinju* arose as a form of desperate resistance and opposition to a civilization that negated humanity.

The prohibition of *junshi* or self-immolation had dealt a mortal blow to the samurai's moral code of honor. This inhuman practice of trying to follow one's master even beyond the grave should not have been permitted at all, but its prohibition confronted feudalism with a dilemma.

During the period of warfare that lasted for nearly a century, it was perhaps a logical requirement that a samurai should be ready to die for his master. These vassals played for high stakes on the battlefield: their own welfare and that of their children. "To die in the presence of his master's horse" was a favorite phrase that stirred the samurai's ambition, for his offspring would be honored by

---

*Wada Katsunari: *Philosophy of Seppuku*, P. 148–9.

his master and his master's heirs, if he were to fall in battle.

When peace was finally ushered in under the prodigious generalship of Tokugawa Ieyasu, there were no more such stages for glory; they could no longer "die in the presence of their master's horse." However, down through the time of the Second and even the Third Shogun, there were still generals alive who could not forget past glories in battle. It was understandable why those lords and generals wanted to practice *junshi* when the Second and Third Shogun died. These were rare opportunities "to die in the presence of the master's horse." To them, loyalty without death was meaningless; there was art even in loyalty.

It was important that the Tokugawa Shogunate had so many loyal lords who would gladly give up their lives, but it was a shocking phenomenon of the feudal system itself that the vassals who composed such an asset to the Shogunate had to die when there was no war. This devotion, lofty as it was, only served to weaken the state. Feudalism itself was designed for war, not peace.

This was the fundamental dilemma. Moreover, there were certainly some leaders in the Shogunate system who had awakened to a more humanistic mode of thinking. Finally there came about, under the leadership of such elements, the prohibition of the practice of self-immolation in 1663. It could not have been otherwise. In a sense, it was official recognition that seppuku had lost its *raison d'être*.

Thereafter, seppuku no longer meant a living sacrifice for a lofty cause, but only a somewhat honorable punishment. Together with the long peace, this situation invited demoralization of the samurai class to the extent that many of the younger ones wore fancy clothes, and effete indulgence held sway over the whole country, especially in Edo. The Genroku* Period was most notable for this tendency. The economic rise of the *chonin* class spurred on this situation all the more.

True, the code of seppuku was taught all this while; the highest glory for the samurai was still to dedicate his soul and body to his lord. But that opportunity seldom, if ever, came, and, thus, the solemn teachings became only empty words.

Germs of Humanity in Battle Records

The feudal ideology was built on a basis of artificial social relations. Therefore, it is quite conceivable that such a system would sooner or later run afoul of basic human nature, leading to its dissolution.

It is interesting to study a few examples of the historical writings from the formative periods of feudalistic morality, decidedly showing a changing faith.

Kajiwara Kagetoki, a distinguished commander, had two sons, Genta and Saburo. Commanding an infantry troop of five hundred, he invaded the enemy's camp. After withdrawal, Genta was not to be found. "Where is he?" Kagetoki asked. "Probably he pressed too deeply into the

---

*It was during this period (in its fourteenth year) that the 47 *ronin* chose to die for their master, while other samurai were imitating the luxurious effeteness of the *chonin*.

enemy's ranks; he may have fallen, for he is nowhere to be seen," answered one of his vassals. Kagetoki, shedding tears, said, "Do you know why I risk myself in war? It is only for the sake of my sons. If Genta is slain, there is little reason for me to live." So saying, he again attacked the enemy, leading on to great deeds.

The gallant fighting of Kagetoki was not motivated by loyalty to his master, but appears to have been for the sake of his sons. Here he was in conflict with the code of the samurai. Though his rashness coincidentally led on to great deeds, we find his human emotions in conflict with the ways of feudalism.

During the strife of the Hogen Period, when the whole Minamoto family was split into two factions, Tametomo, the youngest son and a great archer, was about to loose an arrow at his eldest brother, Yoshitomo. At the critical moment, the latter cried, "Wait, I will propose a bargain. If you are defeated, I will save your life; if my side is defeated, I will ask you to save my life!" Tametomo agreed and lowered his bow. Such bargaining, even between brothers, was not in keeping with the rigid feudal code.

Pursuing a defeated troop of Heike soldiers at the Ichi-no-tani Citadel, Kumagai Jiro Noanzane spurred his horse up to the beach, thinking that the Heike leaders would escape to sea by jumping into boats moored along the shore of Suma. He sighted an imposing samurai, wearing a golden sword, riding into the sea to catch one of the boats that was already afloat. Kumagai called to him, challenging him to a duel. Hating to be thought a coward, the Heike warrior plunged back to the beach, where

Kumagai was waiting. After fighting a short while, the Heike warrior suddenly appeared quite tired. Resigning himself, he removed his helmet and requested Kumagai to cut off his head. To Kumagai's surprise, he was a handsome boy of about sixteen. Kumagai's thoughts turned to his own son of the same age; when the latter suffered a slight wound that same morning, how worried he had been! If this young warrior were killed, how his parents would grieve! He was tempted to be merciful. But then it was too late! His own troop came riding up to him. Fearing to be thought soft or traitorous, he swiftly cut off the head of this young, handsome samurai. After this, he renounced the world and became a monk.

Kumagai, although he succeeded in avoiding the betrayal of his faction, almost succumbed to humane feelings. At least in his mind, feudalism was losing its hold.

Disintegration from Within

Peace lasted for nearly 300 years during the Edo Period, and feudal society flourished. But, even while thriving, it began to show indications of its eventual dissolution. The elements contributory to this disintegration are significant.

Peace enhanced commerce and artisanship and commoners began to accumulate wealth. Inflated finances, aggravated by the introduction of luxuries, gradually lowered the living standards of the samurai class in general. The policy taken by the Shogunate to cope with this situation was the same as that taken by some feudal lords in

Europe: onerous taxation, prohibitive edicts against effete ways, recoinage, loans from commoners, etc. None of these methods, however, afforded a fundamental solution to the ever worsening feudal economy. Finally, the stipends of their vassals were borrowed against by the lords, which was, of course, tantamount to reducing the stipends. Poverty among the samurai prevailed everywhere, which was, no doubt, contributory to bringing about their distrust of the feudal system. The samurai class of this period was completely separated from the land, in contrast to that of the Kamakura Period. They were reduced to the status of mere "salarymen."

Swordsmanship did nothing to assist them financially in an age of peace. A talent for business began to mean something, even among the samurai. Such economic pressures gradually eroded the samurai spirit.

A famous physician, Sugita Gempaku, of the Edo Period, left the following criticism:

> Living under an auspicious reign for nearly two hundred and fifty years, chivalry has dwindled away, and even the direct feudatorial *samurai* and other high retainers, in seven cases out of ten, are dressed like women; far from entertaining noble ambitions, they behave like merchants; the *samurai* now know no shame.

The ruling samurai class could not compete with the economic power of the merchant class and thus began the rise of the commoner. Destitute lords, in exchange for loans from wealthy merchants, gave them the privilege of wearing swords. Commoners wearing swords! Feudal dignity was offended.

Clever samurai married daughters of wealthy merchants, and other samurai pretended not to be envious.

The drastic edict of prohibition against *oibara* or self-immolation was the first and most decisive display of humanism in the comparatively early days of the Tokugawa reign. The following humanistic expression found in *Hihon Tamakushige* is worthy of notice:

> However courageous it may be to perform *seppuku*, the custom is not a recommendable one. Not only is a life lost, but also it is a pity to cause one's parents, wife, and children bitter grief. His Late Excellency Ietsuna, the Fourth *Shogun*, prohibited self-immolation. Your Excellency too should strictly prohibit all kinds of *seppuku*.

This was humanitarian advice, and it endangered Bushido. Such ideas must have been held by many others, though none of them left their views in writing for posterity.

The custom of *shinju* did much damage to the cause of feudalism. Under the feudal system, one married to beget issue who in turn would continue to serve the feudal lord. Therefore, choosing a bride was not a job for a young, inexperienced man; it was presumed that the parents would choose the best partner for their son. True love and romance played no part in this scheme of things.

Opposition to this suppression of the freedom to love whom one pleased was expressed by *shinju*, where the lovers put themselves beyond the control of society.

Not only was *shinju* a denial of feudal authority, but, when it was done by a samurai and a woman, it also meant a significant change in basic attitudes. In the Japanese code of Bushido, there is the inherent disdain of women (an influence of Confucianism) which is quite different from European chivalry. It is remarkable that some men, however few, were brave enough to love as they pleased in such a social and educational environment. A poignant example was that of Fujita Geki. Born into a house that was a direct feudatory vassal of the Tokugawa Shogun, he was heir to an annual income of 5,000 *koku** of rice. He fell in love with a geisha named Ayaginu and they committed *shinju* in a farmhouse. A popular song about his tragic romance had a wide circulation in Edo:

> *Shall I bide with you?*
> *Or take the stipend of*
> *Five thousand, which will it be?*
> *—Better to bide with you!*

On the other hand, protesting voices were raised against the declining morals of the samurai. Yamaoka Shummei, in his book, writes:

> It is the grand age of peace. People neglect, therefore, warlike preparations, looking upon the ancient facts of seppuku or self-immolation as hateful affairs. To my narrow knowledge, I never hear of a man these days who attempts to investigate such matters. Even if there were such a man, there would be no one who knows enough to teach him.

However, the awakening of humanism among the samurai class itself, as well as financial distress enhanced by inflation caused by commercial prosperity on the part

---

*A lord's rank in the hierarchy was shown by the amount of rice his fief produced. One *koku* is 4.9629 bushels.

of the merchants, were contributory to lessening the confidence of the ruling class.

A contemporary *senryu* poem (see footnote, related comments on page 88) eloquently caricatured the plight of the samurai:

> *The samurai will use*
> *A toothpick even if he hasn't dined!*

Decline of Bushido

Dr. Erwin Baelz refers to the essence of Bushido as a severance of emotion from intellect. By this, he means to explain the enigma of the samurai's stoic composure in the face of death by saying that the samurai was able to repress his emotions. However, this view may be disputed. Under the feudal social order, reasoning, i.e., intellect, was not allowed, because it could lead to last-minute rebellions. What was expected of the samurai was "dedicated loyalty" and "filial piety." Any order or statement of the master or father was exempt from critical judgment. Only blind obedience was required. The edicts of the lord were to be obeyed. They brought boon or disaster to the fief or cause.

These edicts of "shalt" and "shalt not" were, after all, based on only the will of the respective lords, and not on the ethical sciences or inherent human reason. In extreme forms, they were nothing more than a sort of madness that excluded critical judgments of value.

A strikingly extreme view along this line can be found in

a volume entitled *Hagakure*. According to its writer:

> *Bushido* means to die insane. Great deeds of *Bushido* cannot be done if one is sound in mind. Just go mad, and die mad. Moreover, if a *samurai* rises to the level where he can discern good and evil, he will not be able to do great work, because he will know the uses of fear. Don't think of loyalty or filial duty. Just die mad. In so doing, the causes of loyalty and duty to the master will be served.

This particular line of reasoning, or rather *a priori* theory, goes a step further to say that even to choose the time and place for one's own death was wrong and that a desire for fame and high reputation was evil. *Hagakure* sharply criticized the otherwise highly lauded vendetta and death of the 47 *ronin* who took revenge for the death of their abused master, pointing out that their methods were in conflict even with their own code of Bushido. However, historian Ishida Bunshiro criticizes this dissenting view and calls it an isolated prejudice.

The opposing point of view taken by *Hagakure* becomes even more remarkable when one realizes that it was written in the latter part of the Tokugawa Era, when Bushido had attained its zenith.

A lack of fear of death was one of the major pillars in the moral code of the samurai. Numerous books were written contributory to refining and elevating this view. At no other time in the history of Japan was theorizing and speculation about death so widespread as in this period.

Both *Hagakure* and another work, *Nabeshima Rongo*, state that "Bushido is nothing but a road to death."

Yamaga Soko, the famous teacher of military science for

the 47 *ronin*, also taught the samurai to concentrate and meditate on death. In the same view *Hagakure* states that the "spirit of Bushido is realized when one imagines himself to be dying; this he can do every morning and every evening." Yamamoto Tsunetomo, the author of *Hagakure*, wrote, "One should expect death daily, so, when the time comes, he can die in peace. Calamity, when it occurs, is not so dreadful as was feared. It is foolish to torment one's self beforehand with vain imaginings. Be resigned always to the thought that the fate of a servant (that is, samurai) is either to become a *ronin* or to commit seppuku."

He goes on, "Tranquilize your mind every morning, and imagine the moment when you may be torn and mangled by arrows, guns, lances, and swords, swept away by great waves, thrown into a fire, struck down by thunderbolts, shaken by earthquakes, falling from a precipice, dying of disease, or dead from an unexpected accident: die every morning in your mind, and then you will not fear death!"

As can be seen in the foregoing, the attitude gradually moved away from the original idea of loyalty to the master for the sake of great military accomplishment. It proceeded down the speculative road toward the "metaphysics of death." Increasingly in proportion to this tendency, the act of seppuku was transformed into a ceremony accompanied by complicated formalities.

Thus, the role played by seppuku became so vital that it came to be called "the flower of *Bushido*." Therefore, mental preparedness for seppuku (and death) as well as the acquisition of a knowledge of the ceremonial techniques became mandatory for samurai. In samurai families, therefore, this vital instruction began in early childhood.

The Gempuku Ceremony

Children of samurai were brought up to believe that one's life is not for one's self. When they reached the age of seven, boys were given a *wakizashi* or short sword, while girls were given a short dirk as protection. They were repeatedly instructed to behave in compliance with the code. When a boy became fifteen, he was given both long and short swords in a solemn ceremony, simultaneously being taught the meaning of these swords. How cynical it was that these swords were often not used against an enemy but against himself. If a women had to kill herself to protect her chastity, she dressed as for her wedding, and then cut the carotid artery in her throat.

With this rite of *gempuku*, boys were initiated to adulthood. The first thing taught at this ceremony was how to commit seppuku and how to draw the dirk out from the right abdomen and then up to cut the carotid artery.

The story of Taira-no-Munemori, a young general of the Heike, was long told to the children of samurai as an example they should not emulate.

When Minamoto-no-Yoritomo captured Taira-no-Munemori, who also held a ministership in the Imperial Household, the former wanted to avoid a direct order of decapitation, so he had a large carp laid out on a chopping board together with a dirk, thus suggesting self-destruction at Taira's own initiation. Taira did not understand this hint from Yoritomo and he struggled against death up to the last moment. This tale of his cowardice was often told to urge the children of samurai to accept death bravely when it was their lot.

Criticism by Commoners

Criticism of the ways of the samurai began to rise during the Edo Period among the class of commoners called *chonin*.

In the Edo days, a satirical style of poetry called *senryu** came into being, and is popular even now. It is a precise style in which each poem is comprised of seventeen syllables that are divided into lines of five, seven, and five syllables respectively. One of them runs like this: "Teaching cutting/The abdomen, they love . . ."

It was intended as sharp satire that the samurai who supposedly loved their children, taught them how to kill themselves. Since open criticism of the samurai by commoners was dangerous, such *senryu* were a means of resistance against the inhumane code of Bushido. Considering the extremely weak standing of the commoners, the *senryu* were a brave attempt to direct criticism against the ruling classes.

Wada Katsunari, in his *Philosophy of Seppuku*, interprets the foregoing poem as a eulogy in praise of the samurai education, but the historical trend of *senryu* will

*Similar to the form of the better known haiku, *senryu* differs in intent.

not permit this interpretation. It is not a style for eulogy, but for satire and indirect resistance against feudal authority. Wada's interpretation becomes insupportable when these reasons are considered. Moreover, the humor would be lost if Wada's view were accepted, and satirical humor is the essence of *senryu*.

V

REVIVAL OF SEPPUKU

An Imperfect Renovation

THE THIRTY years following 1868 were an important period for Japan, during which she emerged as a modern state. The beginning of this new age is known as the Meiji *Ishin* or the Meiji Renovation. It is more commonly known as the "Meiji Restoration" from the fact that hegemony was restored to the Emperor. As an age of national reorientation, it was certainly a "renovation," but from the retrospective point of view, it was indeed a "restoration."

Granting its great attainments, the Meiji Renovation was nevertheless an imperfect one. The overwhelming tide of foreign influence actually did not allow Japan adequate time to modernize thoroughly the structure of the state. In June, 1853, Commodore Matthew Calbraith Perry of the U. S. anchored off Uraga with a fleet of four warships, carrying an official communication from President Fillmore. Perry again came to Japan the following year with seven warships, and Japan was obliged to conclude a treaty and to open two ports, Shimoda and Hakodate.

One month after the first visit of Commodore Perry, there came a Russian Admiral, Eufimii Wassilievitch Putiatin, to Nagasaki with four warships, requesting a treaty as well as a fixing of the border within Saghalin. Then there came a considerable competition among the powers —Britain, Holland, France, etc.—who rushed to Japan one after the other to conclude treaties. Aroused from its long isolation, Japan became a busy center of international affairs.

Thus pressed by the great powers, Japan did not have adequate time to overhaul properly the feudalistic system of the state.

At the same time, the Meiji Government had to persuade the old feudatories to submit to modernization by offers of suitable compensation for power and property forfeited. All feudal lords, far from being demoted or banished, received honorable treatment and were granted titles, together with the Court nobles.

In effect, the Meiji Renovation was an entity born of compromise between modern parliamentarianism and old feudalism. Feudalistic remnants held over by the Meiji Government formed the foundation of the modern state. To a degree, the international situation in the Far East afforded a justification for this militarism. Russian ambitions in Korea and Manchuria appeared on the horizon just as Japan was modernizing its army and navy.

Moreover, as the rapidly growing modern industries of Japan needed the China market, the military power was required to enter this market in competition with the great powers, who maintained military forces in China.

Unification of Objects of Loyalty

During the feudal age, one's loyalty was directed toward his own master, and loyalty objects were multiplex. The Meiji Restoration, however, concentrated this loyalty on one point of focus: the Emperor. Titles without concomitant privileges were given to the older class of samurai, called *shizoku;* otherwise, all the people received equal treatment in the new military order—there were neither samurai nor *chonin*.

The Imperial Rescript to Military Men of 1882 was an epoch-making revitalization of Bushido, in which all the major teachings of Bushido of the past were included in essence. It ran, in abbreviated form, as follows:

> The military man's first duty is to be loyal.
> The military man shall be upright in his demeanor.
> The military man shall highly esteem health and strength.
> The military man shall esteem fidelity.
> The military man shall make frugality a basic principle.

All soldiers conscripted from the people were obliged to memorize this code. Whereas the philosophy of Bushido was taught to the elite only during the Edo Period, this Imperial Rescript influenced the whole nation.

Military officers were forbidden to interfere in politics.

At this point, the Bushido of the Meiji Era was purer than the older variety. It was the violation of this principle that plunged Japan into a disastrous war.

Speculation About Bushido

In the late 1880's, a class of people called *Nippon-shugi-sha* (people who believed in Japan's divinely ordained leading place among nations) began to appear. These people became very active and vocal after the victories Japan won in the Sino-Japanese War (1894–5) and the Russo-Japanese War (1904–5). This rising nationalism and expansionism encouraged the revival of Bushido.

From this period on, books about Bushido appeared one after the other. The first and best-known internationally was that of Dr. Inazo Nitobe, written in English under the title of *Bushido* (1899) with the intent of letting foreigners know what Bushido is. A steady flow of books on the subject followed in rapid succession.

Aside from these books, popular amusements such as *naniwa-bushi*, (a kind of intonated recital), *kodan* (story-narration), and kabuki contributed to teaching the historical tales based on Bushido, thus influencing the masses.

Modern Seppuku

Two dominant principles flowed through from the Meiji Renovation on. One was the ideology built around worship of the Emperor which was a centralized-authoritarian-state ideology with expansionist tendencies. The other ideology supported the people's liberties and rights, that is, constitutionalism. The former carried the strong reaction to feudalism, while the latter, of course, was democratic. These two ideologies, combined as they were under a single regime, caused sporadic conflicts throughout the course of modern politics in Japan.

In the second year of the Meiji Restoration, an important conference was held to discuss Japan's future course. One of the attendees, named Ono Seigoro, proposed to abolish the custom of seppuku. Out of 206 persons, 197 voted against this proposal. Three supported it, and six abstained from voting. The reasons given for opposition were:

1. Seppuku is the shrine of the national spirit and is, in itself, a moral act.
2. It is a great ornament to the Empire.
3. It is a supporting pillar of the national policy.
4. It will nourish the pure pursuit of honor; it will simultaneously be the source of a flow of beautiful emotion as found in the samurai class, which is itself a supporting pillar of the nation.
5. It is a spur to religious sentiment and to moral aspirations.

Not only was Ono opposed by the majority in his bold proposal but he was also assassinated soon afterward.

The abolition of seppuku was frequently proposed and promoted in various circles; in the new criminal code promulgated in 1870, the word seppuku was simply altered to *jisai* (self-disposal). It was therein stipulated that the children of samurai, that is, the *shizoku*, alone would be permitted to dispose of themselves and that their heirs would continue to receive the hereditary stipends.

In the later-revised criminal code (1873), life imprisonment was substituted for *jisai*. With that, seppuku (and *jisai*) permanently disappeared from the penal code of Japan.

Even after the samurai caste was abolished, a man by the name of Kumoi Tatsuo conspired with scores of former samurai to revive the feudal *bakufu* or Shogunate, but failed. Another alarming retrogression was seen in the 9th year of Meiji. A revolt took place in Kumamoto by a fanatic group called the Shimpuren (God-wind League) who opposed the edict abolishing the wearing of swords. They were beaten down but it showed how tenacious remnants of feudalism struggled against the modernization of Japan.

Slowly and gradually seppuku disappeared, at least as an official method of punishment. However, cases of individual seppuku continued until even recent years. As long as there are devotees of Bushido, its flower may bloom. The following examples suggest this:

Around the 13th year of Meiji (1880), the movement to establish a parliament was started. Arguments in the newspapers* grew more heated day by day. The advocates and dissidents, coming to Tokyo from the rural areas carrying placards with written opinions, were innumerable. The government tried to suppress these movements, and

---

*The newspaper men, especially the editors and columnists, were often from the former samurai class.

sporadic violence occurred. There were some who killed themselves at the height of the trouble. One disemboweled himself and while dying, painted the rising sun on a piece of white cloth with his blood and held it aloft.

On August 18 of the same year, a military man committed seppuku at the front gate of the temporary Imperial residence in Akasaka. This news was disseminated widely. Being a corporal of the First Regiment in Tokyo, he was carrying a letter to the Minister of the Imperial Household. One month after his death, a letter to his mother was brought to light, which said in part:

> ... These days, those who follow the Imperial instructions are anxious about the situation that prevails in our country. They come to Tokyo to appeal to the government for the establishment of a parliament. The government should consider their supplications. Not only does it not do so but it tries to repress these loyal persons. There can be no greater regret. I have decided to encourage these supplicants by sacrificing my own self. I am sorry to be lacking in filial duty to my benevolent mother. However, if a parliament is not set up, both the people as well as the Emperor will have trouble in days to come ...

Then there was the self-immolation of General and Mrs. Nogi who committed suicide according to the code of Bushido when Emperor Meiji passed away in 1912.

Professor Tanimoto Yutaka of the Tokyo Imperial University, a Doctor of Literature, sharply criticized them for this and as a result, was expelled from the university. From that time until the end of World War II, it was taboo to criticize General and Mrs. Nogi. The General was enshrined as a god of war, and his memory was much utilized for the purposes of ultra-nationalistic education.

Another case which received wide publicity was that of a youth who assassinated a high official. Stirred up by the murder of a Japanese during a revolution in China, the China situation was fiercely debated in 1913. On September 5, Abe Moritaro, Director of the Political Affairs Bureau of the Foreign Ministry, was assassinated. The assassin was a youth of eighteen, carrying a statement called a *zankanjo* (a written vindication of an assassin's deed) as well as a letter directed to a certain lawyer, into whose house he fled and committed seppuku, on a map of China. In the suicide note to his parents, this young assassin wrote:

> The existence of Abe is a great loss to the country. If I now assassinate him, the whole nation, including the Foreign Ministry, will awaken, especially the officials with wrong notions. Moreover, I can quicken the awakening of the young people. My single life is almost nothing in comparison to my contribution in defending our country . . .
> . . . I don't want to cause any further trouble and so I will disembowel myself according to the traditional rites, thus dedicating myself to His Imperial Majesty.

When the U.S. Senate passed the Immigration Bill in April, 1924, indignant cries were raised in various parts of Japan. A certain man, carrying a suicide note addressed to the American people and calling himself an anonymous citizen of the Japanese Empire, disemboweled himself in front of the U.S. Embassy. The letter read:

> Taking advantage of the fact that Your Excellency, Ambassador Siras E. Woods, has a deep understanding of and sympathy towards Japan, I want to request your good

offices in calling forth a profound soul-searching by all the American people.

His message was:

> Please eliminate the anti-Japanese stipulations from the new Immigration Law. Whereas America occupies an important position as an advocate of peace from the humanistic point of view, I am dumbfounded to see the inhuman, anti-Japanese bill passed by both Houses. I had better die to study the universal love that America has proclaimed, to listen to the words of Christ [he was a Christian], to call forth deep soul searching on the part of your people, and to pray for the happiness of America. It is better to thus die than to hold rancor in myself against America.

Lieutenant Colonel Kuga Noboru, a military officer taken captive, killed himself on the battlefield at Howanchin in China in an unusual case of seppuku. He was seriously wounded by a bullet and fell unconscious. When he came to, he found himself a prisoner. He found that his pistol was still on his person, undiscovered by his captors, and he used it to commit suicide. In his farewell note, he wrote:

> In destroying myself, I wanted to commit *seppuku*, according to the rites of *Bushido*. However, the blade of my sword was bent during the fight and I could not withdraw it from its scabbard. Hence I was obliged to use my pistol against my wishes.

In his death poem, called *jisei*, he said he would go the way of samurai, observing the teachings of his father. Shanghai Military Headquarters announced his death, in accordance with his desires, using the terminology *jijin*, which suggests the use of a sword in taking one's own life.

On the same day of the Pearl Harbor attack, a steamer, the 5,000-ton "Nagasaki-Maru," met the mammoth s. s. "President Harrison" (15,000 tons) on the China Sea and captured her after pursuing her for eleven hours. The captain, Suga Genzaburo, made himself famous by this exploit. Five months later, his ship sank off Nagasaki after striking a mine. A week later, he performed seppuku, because his ship was a total loss. He cut his abdomen crosswise with a razor and then his carotid artery in four places. A policeman who inspected his corpse exclaimed in admiration, "I have never seen such a heroic seppuku. And look how peacefully he sleeps! He is almost godlike!"

Despite the elimination of seppuku from the legal codes early in the Meiji Renovation, it never ceased to occur, especially during World War II, when the spirit of Bushido was strongly emphasized. Many cases of seppuku occurred on the mainland as well as on isolated islands in the South Seas. The *kami-kaze* attacks were in themselves manifestations of Bushido.

When unconditional surrender was announced on 15 August, 1945, General Anami, then the Army Minister, disemboweled himself, and other ultra-nationalistic military officers followed suit on the Palace Plaza, facing the Imperial Household. On the drill-field at Yoyogi, later called Washington Heights, ten military men disemboweled themselves while cursing the military forces of the U.S.

Oddly enough, Bushido reached its zenith, in a sense, after feudalism was abolished at the start of the Meiji Restoration. Main factors contributing to this were the concentration of loyalty on the Emperor, the enactment of the conscription law (leveling the difference between samurai and *chonin*), and the Imperial Rescript to Military Men which helped to strengthen the code of Bushido among soldiers and sailors.

Downfall of Bushido

Japan had fought China for nine years and other great powers for five years until she surrendered in 1945. The militarism of Japan, with its thousand years of history, was defeated. Bushido appeared to have been completely eradicated.

The deep and general conviction of defeat among the people and the comparative success of the American Occupation policies served to wipe out the last traces of Bushido. Japan had never before been completely defeated and the effect on the Japanese mentality was extremely profound. A feeling somewhat akin to religious resignation dominated the minds of the people. Everything belonging to the militaristic past was abhorred.

This abhorrence of war was subtly utilized in the Occupation policies. A quiet but thorough social revolution was wrought. Under the Occupation, headed by General MacArthur, severe blows were dealt to the traditional nationalism of Japan. The most important single factor was the declaration by the Emperor of non-divine status. Others were the prohibition of the reading of the Imperial Rescript for Education in schools, the implantation of democracy, and the constitutional renunciation of war.

General MacArthur demanded that the Emperor deny his divinity, but it must be remembered that it was not the wish of the Emperor that he be thought a god. Rather, this was the work of militarists and ultra-Shintoists. The Emperor at first declined to make the demanded declaration. However, when he did, it had a profound influence on the reorientation of the national spirit of Japan. Primary school education was shaken to its foundations, and is still not too well ordered.

The Imperial Rescript for Education read in all schools had been the supporting pillar of Japanese education since 1890. The principles flowing through the Rescript are a blend of Shintoistic national history and Confucianism. Prohibiting its reading caused the teaching of Confucianism, directly or indirectly, to be removed from national education.

Nor did the edicts stop there. What was most feared was a revival of militarism. Previously, all main shrines throughout Japan were government supported. Now, they lost their annual subsidies by command of SCAP (Supreme Commander for the Allied Powers). Christianity, which had been repressed from time to time, was assured freedom of activity. The underlying purpose was to assist the spread of Christianity, while discouraging the nationalistic religion of Shinto.

In destroying the ultra-nationalism of prewar Japan, the Occupation enjoyed almost complete success.

Along with that, there was an implantation of democracy

REVIVAL OF SEPPUKU 103

in the Japanese mind. Thoroughgoing democratization was carried out in all governmental offices, and most civil organizations followed suit.

The promulgation of the new Constitution was an epoch-making event of the Occupation. In Article 9 of Chapter II, the Japanese people took a step revolutionary among modern, civilized nations: They decided to ". . . forever renounce war as a sovereign right of the nation and the threat or use of force as a means of settling international disputes." Although this stipulation is part of a document formulated under the guidance of SCAP's Government Section, it stands nonetheless as a tribute to man's aspirations.

It also lowers the final curtain on Bushido. The protagonists, some in the garb of samurai and others in the uniforms of *kami-kaze* pilots, have left the stage, with the underlying theme symbolized in the cherry blossom insignia: Live briefly but gloriously. One's evanescent life is but a preparation for death. The fall of the blossom is as moving as its beauty on the limb and the final moment, ceremonialized in the ritual of seppuku, is indeed the moment of truth!

GLOSSARY

ashigaru: literally, light footed; a foot soldier; a lower-ranking samurai.

azukari-nin: caretaker of seppuku ceremony.

bakufu: the Shogunate government of feudal Japan.

bushi: warrior; samurai.

Bushido: the code of the samurai of Japan.

byobu: a folding, standing screen.

choku: small sake cup.

chonin: merchant.

chugi-bara: hara-kiri to show loyalty to one's master.

daimyo: feudal lord.

daki-kubi: technique of "retaining the head" in decapitation by leaving a portion of uncut skin at the throat so that the head would not roll away but would hang down.

doshin: constable.

funshi: seppuku caused by indignation.

futon: comforter, heavy quilt.

gempuku: rite celebrating a boy's attaining "adulthood" observed at age fifteen.

hakama: formal trousers.

haniwa: clay statues of persons and animals buried with their masters in lieu of living creatures.

hara: abdomen.

hara-kiri: cutting the abdomen.

hatamoto: a direct feudatory of the Shogun.

hina: a doll.

hito-bashira: human pillar.

jijin: to commit suicide with a sword.

jisai: self-destruction.

jisei: death poem.

jumonji: crosswise cut.

junshi: to follow one's master in death.

joruri: a kind of ballad-drama, using puppets (Awaji is is the home of this form of theater in Japan).

kabuki: the classical theater of Japan.

kaishaku: assisting at seppuku.

kaishaku-nin: the assistant at seppuku.

kami-kaze: literally, divine wind. In World War II, the

pilots of the Special Attack Corps who dove their bomb-laden planes into U.S. navy craft.

kamishimo: old ceremonial dress with high winglike shoulders.

kana: the Japanese syllabary as differentiated from the more difficult Chinese ideographs (*kanji*).

kanji: the Chinese ideographs which form the base of the written Japanese language.

kanshi: hara-kiri for purpose of remonstration.

karo: principle retainers.

kataginu: ensemble of *kamishimo* and *hakama*.

kenshi: inspector dispatched to observe seppuku ceremonies.

kiru, kiri: to cut, cutting.

kodan: storytelling.

koku: a unit of weight; 4.9629 bushels.

kombu: kelp or seaweed.

kozuka: a small blade.

kubi-shozoku: dressing of the decapitated head.

kun: native Japanese style of pronouncing Chinese written character (see also *on*).

matsugo-no-mizu: literally, water for the last moment.

metsuke: supreme judge; also, *ometsuke* (the "o" is honorific).

Mikado: the Japanese Emperor; a word seldom used by the Japanese.

mikire: literally, three slices; also, to cut flesh.

mujoki: white streamers ("banners of heartlessness").

munen-bara: hara-kiri from mortification.

naniwa-bushi: a kind of recital.

nehan-mon: Nirvana gate.

oibara: suicide to follow one's deceased master.

on: Japanese rendering of Chinese reading of Chinese written character (see also *kun*).

otoshi-zashi: method of carrying sword by attaching to the belt.

o-zen: small raised tray for individual dining.

raise: the next world or life.

rochu: feudal cabinet; also, member of this body.

ronin: warrior without a master.

rusui-yaku: custodian of seppuku ceremony.

sake: rice-wine.

sambo: offering tray.

samurai: warrior.

sanzoku: mountain bandit.

senryu: a satirical poem.

seppuku: self-disembowelment.

seppuku-mono: idiom meaning situation calling for seppuku.

shaku: a unit of measurement; 11.93 inches.

shi: four; also, the root of the word meaning death.

shinju: literally, revealing the heart; suicide by two lovers.

shizoku: a descendant of a samurai.

shogun: a generalissimo; the *de facto* military rulers of Japan during the feudal period.

shugenja: an ascetic hermit of the mountains.

shugyo-mon: ascetic gate.
shushi: ethics.
sokotsu-shi: expiatory seppuku.
sugihara: a type of Japanese tissue paper.
sun: a unit of measurement; 1.193 inches or one-tenth of a *shaku*.
suzuri: the ink slab used in Japanese calligraphy.
tachi: the long sword of the samurai.
tachi-oshiki: thin wooden plate with four long legs.
tatami: a reed mat three by six feet in size.
wakizashi: the short sword of the samurai.
yomi: the "nether world" in Shintoism.
yukaku: the officially licensed gay quarters.
zankanjo: an assassin's written vindication of his deed.
Zen: a sect of Buddhism.
zori: straw sandals.

BIBLIOGRAPHY

Fujita, Toko: *Kodokan Kijutsu Gi* (The Significance of the Kodokan Narrative). A scroll believed to have been written in the 19th century, currently in Ueno Library, Tokyo.

Hojo, Chikuho: *Shido Kokoroe Sho* (The Book of Knowledge of Bushido). Reproduced in the 6th Volume of the *Nihon Kokusui Zensho* (Japan National Purity Collection). 1929.

Ishida, Bunshiro: *Nippon Bushido-shi no Taikeiteki Kenkyu* (Systematic Research into the History of Japanese Bushido). Kinseisha, Tokyo.

Kojima: *Taiheiki* (Chronicles of War). Forty scrolls believed written by a bonze named Kojima who began this work in 1368.

KUDO, YUKIHIRO: *Jijinroku* (Notes on Self-Destruction). 1840.

MATSUOKA, YUKIYOSHI: *Teijo Zakki* (Miscellaneous Notes of Teijo). Unpublished manuscript in 16 scrolls, currently in Ueno Library, Tokyo.

MURDOCH, JAMES: *A History of Japan.* Three volumes. Routledge & Kegan Paul, Ltd., London, 1949.

NITOBE, INAZO: *Bushido, The Soul of Japan.* Shokwabo, Tokyo, 1900.

OGINO, YOSHIYUKI: *Nippon Seido Tsu* (Commentary on Japanese Institutions). Yoshikawa Kobunkan, Tokyo, 1926.

LORD REDESDALE: *Tales of Old Japan.* Reprint edition. Charles E. Tuttle Co., Inc., Tokyo, 1966.

SHIOYA, SAKAE: *Chushingura, An Exposition.* Kenkyusha, Tokyo, 1940.

TOKINAGA, HAMURO: *Hogen Monogatari* (Tales of Hogen). Three scrolls written between 1185 and 1190.

TOKUGAWA, IEYASU: *Goyuijo Hyakkajo* (The One Hundred Articles of Testimony). Sakuhinsha, Tokyo, 1962.

WADA, KATSUNORI: *Seppuku Tetsugaku* (Philosophy of Seppuku). Shubunsha, Tokyo, 1927.

YAMAMOTO, TSUNETOMO: *Hagakure* (In the Shade of the Leaves). Keiei Shicho Kenkyukai, Tokyo, 1964.

YAMANO, SHOTARO: *Nippon Jisatsu Joshiki* (Notes on Suicide in Japan). Kobunsha, Tokyo, 1938.

YAMAOKA, SHUMMEI: *Seppuku Jisatsu Kojitsu no Koto* (Old Facts about Seppuku and Suicide).

INDEX

Abe Moritaro, 98
Anami, General, 100
Asano Takumi-no-Kami, Lord, 52
Ashikaga Takauji, 27, 28

bakufu, 36, 37, 58, 96
beheading, 70
Bizen, 14
Bushido, 11, 12, 32, 45, 76, 82–84, 86, 93, 94, 96, 97, 100, 101, 103
Byodoin, 26

Catholics, 21, 22
Choshiu, 15
chonin, 75, 78, 88, 101
chugi-bara, 32
Chushingura, 53
Confucius, 36, 74, 102
"Cut Off and Bury," 70
"Cut Off and Throw Away," 70

daki-kubi, 60

doshin, 49
double suicide; *see shinju*

Edo, 34, 41–43, 74, 80, 81, 88, 93, 94

fan *hara-kiri*, 69
finger *hara-kiri*, 70
Forty-Seven Loyal Retainers (*var.* 47 *ronin*), 45, 53, 55, 78, 85, 86; *see also, Chushingura*
Fujita Geki, 83
funshi, 39

Gembuku Ceremony, 87
Genji-Heike (Gem-Pei), 11, 20, 34, 35
Godaigo, Emperor 27, 28
Go-Sannen-Gassen (Three-Year War), 26

Hachiman Shrine, 38
Hagakure, 84–86
Haji-no-Omi, 33

hakama, 51, 53, 63, 70
hand *hara-kiri*, 70
haniwa, 33; *see also, yo*
Heimon, 29
Hideyoshi, 21, 39
Hihasu-Hime, Empress, 33
Hissoku, 29
hito-bashira, 24
Hogen Monogatari (Tales of the Hogen Civil War), 25, 26
Hojo, 27
Hokucho, 27
Hosokawa Tsunayoshi, Lord, 45, 46
Hotta Masamori, Lord, 36
Hyogo (*var*. Hiogo), 14, 15

Ichi-no-tani Citadel, 79
Immigration Bill (U.S.), 98
Imperial Rescript on Education, 101, 102
Imperial Rescript to Military Men, 93, 101
Inada Sebei, 37
Inoue, Lord, 43
inspector; *see kenshi*
Ise Anzai, 25
Ishikawa Goemon, 21
Ishikawa Katsuzaemon, 43
Ito Shunsuke, 15
Iwafuji, 24
Izanami, 10

jisai, 95, 96
junshi, 32, 33, 37–39, 76, 77

kabuki, 94
Kai'eki, 29

kaishaku, 16–20, 45, 49, 51, 55, 56, 58–61
Kajiwara Genta, 78
Kajiwara Kagetoki, 78
Kajiwara Saburo, 78
Kamakura, 31, 81
kami-kaze, 100, 103
kamishimo, 50, 51, 63, 70
Kandabashi, 43
kanshi, 32, 38
Kanzanji, 41
karma, 34
karo, 49
kenshi, 46–48, 60, 66
Kira Kozuke-no-suke, 53
kiri-sute, 71
kiri-ume, 71
kodan, 94
Kojiki, 57
kombu, 57
kozuka, 60
kubi-shozoku, 60
Kuga Noboru, Lt. Col., 99
Kumagai Jiro Naonzane, 79
Kumoi Tatsuo, 96
kun, 13; *see also, on*
Kusunoki Masahige, 28
Kusunoki Masasue, 28
Kusunoki Masatsura, 28

MacArthur, General Douglas, 101, 102
Manyoshu, 10
Matsudaira Nobutsuna, Lord, 36
Matsugo-no-mizu, 57
Matsu-no-Roka, 53
Meiji, Emperor, 37, 38, 97
Meiji Restoration, 20, 91–96, 100

INDEX

metsuke, 49
Minamoto-no-Sanetomo, 38
Minamoto-no-Tametomo, 20, 25, 79
Minamoto-no-Tameyoshi, 26
Minamoto-no-Yorimasa, 26
Minamoto-no-Yoshitomo, 79, 87
Minatogawa, 28
Mitford, A.B.; *see*, Redesdale, Lord
mizu-bara, 69
Mori Motonari, 39
Morinaga, Prince, 28
moro-kubi, 70
mujoki, 44
munen-bara, 39
Murakami Yoshiteru, 28
Murasaki, Lady, 11, 74
Muromachi, 34

Nagai, Sir, 41
Nagasaki-maru, 100
Naiki-no-Heita, 26
Naito, Sir, 41
Nan-cho, 26
naniwa-bushi, 94
nahan-mon, 44
Nihon Shoki, 25
Nihon-shugi-sha, 94
Nogi, General, 37, 97
Nomi-no-Sukune, 33

Oda Nobunaga, 38
oibara, 35, 82
on, 9, 13
Ono Seigoro, 95
Otani Sampei, 32
otoshizashi, 66

Otowaka, 26

Perry, Commodore Matthew C., 91, 92
"President Hoover," s.s., 100
Putiatin, Admiral E.W., 92

Redesdale, Lord 14, 19, 20, 47
rochu, 48, 51
rusui-yaku, 47

sake, 54
sam-bo, 57, 65
Satsuma, 15
SCAP, 102, 103
Seifukiji, 15
Sengoku Jidai, 39; *see also* Warfare Period
Sen-no-Rikyu, 39
senryu, 84, 88, 89
sensu-bara, 69
seppuku, 9, 13
shaku, 44
shibari-kubi, 71
Shimizu Muneharu, 39, 40
Shimpukuji, 41
Shimpuren, 96
shinju, 73
Shinryuji, 42
Shinzoin, 46
Shirai, 40
shizoku, 93, 96
Shinto, 10, 42, 102
Shugenja, 45
shugyo-mon, 44
soe-bara, 70
sokotsu-shi, 38
Suga Genzaburo, 100
Sugita Gempaku, 81

Sugiura Uemon-no-Hyoei, 37
Sugiura Zen'eimon, 37

tachi, 66
tachi-tori, 70
Taira-no-Munemori, 87
Taira Teijo, 25
Taki-Zenzaburo, 15, 16, 18
Tale of the Genji, 11, 12, 74
Tamura, Lord, 52
Tanimoto Yutaka, Prof., 97
tatami, 44, 45, 47, 59, 70
te-bara, 70
Toki-no-Juro, 27
Tokugawa, 12, 14, 20, 24, 29, 34, 35, 38, 41, 43, 44, 45, 52, 83; Tokugawa Ietsuna, 61; Tokugawa Ieyasu, 21, 35, 42, 77
toshu, 70

uchi-kubi, 70
Utsunomiya Castle, 37

wakizashi, 17, 50, 66, 87
Wani, 10
Warfare Period, 34, 35, 39, 61, 76
water *hara-kiri*, 69
Woods, Ambassador Siras E., 98
World War II, 38, 100

Yamaga Soko, 85
yo, 36; *see also haniwa*
Yokota Hichijuro, 37
yomi, 23
Yoshino, 27
yubi-bara, 70

zankanjo, 98
Zen, 31
Zojoji, 41

Other TUT BOOKS available:

BACHELOR'S HAWAII *by Boye de Mente*

BACHELOR'S JAPAN *by Boye de Mente*

BACHELOR'S MEXICO *by Boye de Mente*

A BOOK OF NEW ENGLAND LEGENDS AND FOLK LORE *by Samuel Adams Drake*

THE BUDDHA TREE *by Fumio Niwa; translated by Kenneth Strong*

CALABASHES AND KINGS: An Introduction to Hawaii *by Stanley D. Porteus*

CHINA COLLECTING IN AMERICA *by Alice Morse Earle*

CHINESE COOKING MADE EASY *by Rosy Tseng*

CHOI OI!: The Lighter Side of Vietnam *by Tony Zidek*

THE COUNTERFEITER and Other Stories *by Yasushi Inoue; translated by Leon Picon*

CURIOUS PUNISHMENTS OF BYGONE DAYS *by Alice Morse Earle*

CUSTOMS AND FASHIONS IN OLD NEW ENGLAND *by Alice Morse Earle*

DINING IN SPAIN *by Gerrie Beene and Lourdes Miranda King*

EXOTICS AND RETROSPECTIVES *by Lafcadio Hearn*

FIRST YOU TAKE A LEEK: A Guide to Elegant Eating Spiced with Culinary Capers *by Maxine J. Saltonstall*

FIVE WOMEN WHO LOVED LOVE *by Saikaku Ihara; translated by William Theodore de Bary*

A FLOWER DOES NOT TALK: Zen Essays *by Abbot Zenkei Shibayama of the Nanzenji*

FOLK LEGENDS OF JAPAN *by Richard M. Dorson*

GLEANINGS IN BUDDHA-FIELDS: Studies of Hand and Soul in the Far East *by Lafcadio Hearn*

GOING NATIVE IN HAWAII: A Poor Man's Guide to Paradise *by Timothy Head*

HAIKU IN ENGLISH *by Harold G. Henderson*

HARP OF BURMA *by Michio Takeyama; translated by Howard Hibbett*

HAWAII: End of the Rainbow *by Kazuo Miyamoto*

THE HAWAIIAN GUIDE BOOK for Travelers *by Henry M. Whitney*

HAWAIIAN PHRASE BOOK

HISTORIC MANSIONS AND HIGHWAYS AROUND BOSTON *by Samuel Adams Drake*

HISTORICAL AND GEOGRAPHICAL DICTIONARY OF JAPAN *by E. Papinot*

A HISTORY OF JAPANESE LITERATURE *by W. G. Aston*

HOMEMADE ICE CREAM AND SHERBERT *by Sheila MacNiven Cameron*

HOW TO READ CHARACTER: A New Illustrated Handbook of Phrenology and Physiognomy, for Students and Examiners *by Samuel R. Wells*

IN GHOSTLY JAPAN *by Lafcadio Hearn*

INDIAN RIBALDRY *by Randor Guy*

JAPAN: An Attempt at Interpretation *by Lafcadio Hearn*

THE JAPANESE ABACUS *by Takashi Kojima*

THE JAPANESE ARE LIKE THAT *by Ichiro Kawasaki*

JAPANESE ETIQUETTE: An Introduction *by the World Fellowship Committee of the Tokyo Y.W.C.A.*

THE JAPANESE FAIRY BOOK *compiled by Yei Theodora Ozaki*

JAPANESE FOLK-PLAYS: The Ink-Smeared Lady and Other Kyogen *translated by Shio Sakanishi*

JAPANESE FOOD AND COOKING *by Stuart Griffin*

JAPANESE HOMES AND THIER SURROUNDINGS *by Edward S. Morse*

A JAPANESE MISCELLANY *by Lafcadio Hearn*

JAPANESE RECIPES *by Tatsuji Tada*

JAPANESE TALES OF MYSTERY & IMAGINATION *by Edogawa Rampo; translated by James B. Harris*

JAPANESE THINGS: Being Notes on Various Subjects Connected with Japan *by Basil Hall Chamberlain*

THE JOKE'S ON JUDO *by Donn Draeger and Ken Tremayne*

THE KABUKI HANDBOOK *by Aubrey S. Halford and Giovanna M. Halford*

KAPPA *by Ryūnosuke Akutagawa; translated by Geoffrey Bownas*

KOKORO: Hints and Echoes of Japanese Inner Life *by Lafcadio Hearn*

KOREAN FOLK TALES *by Im Bang and Yi Ryuk; translated by James S. Gale*

KOTTŌ: Being Japanese Curios, with Sundry Cobwebs *by Lafcadio Hearn*

KWAIDAN: Stories and Studies of Strange Things *by Lafcadio Hearn*

LET'S STUDY JAPANESE *by Jun Maeda*

THE LIFE OF BUDDHA *by A. Ferdinand Herold*

MODERN JAPANESE PRINTS: A Contemporary Selection *edited by Yuji Abe*

NIHONGI: Chronicles of Japan from the Earliest Times to A.D. 697 *by W. G. Aston*

OLD LANDMARKS AND HISTORIC PERSONAGES OF BOSTON *by Samuel Adams Drake*

ORIENTAL FORTUNE TELLING *by Jimmei Shimano; translated by Togo Taguchi*

PHYSICAL FITNESS: A Practical Program *by Clark Hatch*

READ JAPANESE TODAY *by Len Walsh*

SELF DEFENSE SIMPLIFIED IN PICTURES *by Don Hepler*

SHADOWINGS *by Lafcadio Hearn*

A SHORT SYNOPSIS OF THE MOST ESSENTIAL POINTS IN HAWAIIAN GRAMMAR *by W. D. Alexander*

THE STORY BAG: A Collection of Korean Folk Tales *by Kim So-un; translated by Setsu Higashi*

SUMI-E: An Introduction to Ink Painting *by Nanae Momiyama*

SUN-DIALS AND ROSES OF YESTERDAY *by Alice Morse Earle*

THE TEN FOOT SQUARE HUT AND TALES OF THE HEIKE: Being Two Thirteenth-century Japanese classics, the "Hojoki" and selections from the "Heike Monogatari" *translated by A. L. Sadler*

THIS SCORCHING EARTH *by Donald Richie*

TIMES-SQUARE SAMURAI or the Improbable Japanese Occupation of New York *by Robert B. Johnson and Billie Niles Chadbourne*

TO LIVE IN JAPAN *by Mary Lee O'Neal and Virginia Woodruff*

THE TOURIST AND THE REAL JAPAN *by Boye de Mente*

TOURS OF OKINAWA: A Souvenir Guide to Places of Interest *compiled by Gasei Higa, Isamu Fuchaku, and Zenkichi Toyama*

TWO CENTURIES OF COSTUME IN AMERICA *by Alice Morse Earle*

TYPHOON! TYPHOON! An Illustrated Haiku Sequence *by Lucile M. Bogue*

UNBEATEN TRACKS IN JAPAN: An Account of Travels in the Interior Including Visits to the Aborigines of Yezo and the Shrine of Nikko *by Isabella L. Bird*

ZILCH! The Marine Corps' Most Guarded Secret *by Roy Delgado*

Please order from your bookstore or write directly to:

CHARLES E. TUTTLE CO., INC.
Suido 1-chome, 2–6, Bunkyo-ku, Tokyo 112

or:

CHARLES E. TUTTLE CO., INC.
Rutland, Vermont 05701 U.S.A.